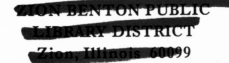

HOW HOLLYWOOD INVENTED
THE WILD WEST

HOLLY GEORGE-WARREN

HOW HOLLYWOOD INVENTED
THE WILD WEST

FEATURING
THE REAL WEST
CAMPFIRE MELODIES
MATINEE IDOLS
FOUR LEGGED FRIENDS
COWGIRLS & LONE GUNS

HOLLY GEORGE-WARREN

Reader's Digest

The Reader's Digest Association, Inc.
Pleasantville, New York/Montreal

For my favorite buckaroos Robert and
Jackson Warren, and for my childhood
cowpoke playmates Owen and Robert George

A READER'S DIGEST BOOK

This edition published by The Reader's Digest Association
by arrangement with
THE IVY PRESS LIMITED
The Old Candlemakers
West Street, Lewes
East Sussex BN7 2NZ, U.K.

Text copyright © Holly George-Warren 2002
Design and layout copyright © The Ivy Press Limited 2002

FOR IVY PRESS
Creative Director Peter Bridgewater
Publisher Sophie Collins
Editorial Director Steve Luck
Design Manager Tony Seddon
Designers David Costa, Emil Dacanay (Wherefore Art?)
Project Editor Caroline Earle
Picture Research Vanessa Fletcher

FOR READER'S DIGEST
Project Editor Nancy Shuker
Project Copy Editor Vicki Fischer
Project Designer George McKeon
Executive Editor, Trade Publishing Dolores York
Senior Design Director Elizabeth Tunnicliffe
Editorial Director Christopher Cavanaugh
Director, Trade Publishing Christopher T. Reggio
Vice President & Publisher, Trade Publishing Harold Clarke

Library of Congress Cataloging-in-Publication Data

George-Warren, Holly.
  Cowboy: how Hollywood invented the Wild West / by Holly George-Warren.
    p. cm.
  Includes index.
  ISBN 0-7621-0375-2
  1. Western films—United States—History and criticism. I. Title.

PN1995.9.W4 G46 2002
791.43'6728—dc21
                                          2002021357

Address any comments about *Cowboy* to:
The Reader's Digest Association, Inc.
Adult Trade Publishing
Reader's Digest Road
Pleasantville, NY 10570-7000

For more Reader's Digest products and information,
visit our website:
www.rd.com (in the United States)
www.readersdigest.ca (in Canada)

Originated and printed by Hong Kong Graphics
and Printing Ltd., China
1 3 5 7 9 10 8 6 4 2

contents

Introduction

WHERE HAVE ALL THE COWBOYS GONE?

INQUIRED ONE OF THE TOP POP SONGS NEAR THE END OF THE TWENTIETH CENTURY. AND AT TIMES, AS THE TWENTIETH CENTURY FADED, IT SEEMED THAT AMERICA'S LEGENDARY HEROES HAD GALLOPED OUT OF SIGHT JUST BEYOND THE HORIZON.

With the birth of the twenty-first century, however, those dashing knights of the plains have been called back into service. They haven't yet made the impact on modern popular culture that they did 100 years ago, giving life to the brand-new motion picture industry, riding on the coattails of the still-solvent but fading traveling Wild West show extravaganzas, and the still-flourishing dime novel publishing boom. As the key figure in all these media, that rugged individualist, the American cowboy, gave us something to aspire to, to dream about, even to use as an excuse.

As the world became morally ambiguous and confusing, though, the cowboy lost his place in it. Screenwriters, movie directors, and actors ran out of new ways to paint his picture with shadows and light. Their audiences looked elsewhere for legendary figures: secret agents, spacemen, superheroes, martial arts specialists.

But as the new millennium dawns, people are calling out for the cowboy again. A battle rages between "good and evil," the likes of which Americans haven't seen since the bombing of Pearl Harbor. People honor heroes who risk their lives to rescue the helpless—heroes who, rather than show up on horseback, arrive on fire engines. Teddy Roosevelt, "the Cowboy President," is back in vogue. The battle over cattle-grazing lands out West has returned to the news.

Will all these political and social events result in the cowboy's returning to the fore in our popular culture? Who's to say? But while we wait for the answer, in this book we travel back to the emergence of the heroic image of the cowboy and trace its spread and ultimate expansion into America's greatest mythic creation. We return to another time—just after the Civil War—when the country was imploding in turmoil. It was during this time that the cowboy came to be. Within just a few years, his reputation would begin to loom larger and larger in the public's imagination: from Buffalo Bill to *The Virginian* to *The Great Train Robbery*, from Tom Mix to the Singing Cowboy, from *The Searchers* to *The Good, the Bad, and the Ugly* to *The Wild Bunch* to *Unforgiven*.

So where have all the cowboys gone? *Cowboy: How Hollywood Invented the Wild West* will show that—at least within our collective identity as Americans—they never really went away....

6

Move 'em out—as late as 1930, cowboys were still at work moving beef on the hoof from the West to the stockyards of Chicago. There was money in them thar cows, or at least in cowboy service industries; the Deadwood Treasure Wagon, shown opposite, was operated by the Wells Fargo company and routinely transferred huge sums in gold bullion from East to West and back again, becoming a prime target for robbers.

Home on the Range
THE GOLDEN AGE OF THE COWBOY

LEAN AND LANKY, SITTING TALL IN THE SADDLE AND WEARING A WHITE HAT, RIDING WILD AND FREE ACROSS THE PLAINS, DEFEATING OUTLAWS AND RESCUING THE DEFENSELESS: SINCE THE 1880S, THIS HAS BEEN THE PREVAILING IMAGE OF THE WILD WEST COWBOY.

How much of this image is reality, and how much is myth created by literature, paintings, movies, songs, and recordings? If we look at the first known usage of the word "cowboy," this picture doesn't ring true

at all. In the 1770s, during the time of the Revolutionary War, "cow boy" was a derogatory term for conniving Tories who devised a scheme for capturing American colonists. Lying in wait in the underbrush, they would ring a bell, then ambush the unsuspecting farmer who ventured out to retrieve a missing heifer. In the nineteenth century, still considered bad guys, "cow boys" were Texas bandits who swiped Mexican cattle. Only after the Civil War did cowboys (sometimes hyphenated or spelled as two words) come to mean the rough-riding men who tended cattle for a living.

It was also during the postwar period that cowboys began to proliferate. The war between the states displaced thousands of Southerners who had lost the family farm and the means to earn a living; some went to Texas to start over. There, thousands of cattle ran loose on the open range. They came from local ranches and farms that had been deserted during the war, and from Mexico, where cattle were raised for leather and tallow rather than for beef.

As far back as the late 1700s, Mexican cattlemen, known as vaqueros, had brought skills for raising their horses, cattle, and livestock to Texas. With ranching traditions, gear, and clothing adapted from Spain, the vaquero was actually the predecessor of the American cowboy; in fact, "buckaroo" was the Anglicized version of the word "vaquero." Much cowboy terminology comes from Spanish words in the Mexican vaquero tradition, including lariat, lasso, roundup, rodeo, corral, chaps, and mustang.

10

A group of original cowboys, Mexican *vaqueros*, shoe a pony. Their skills, as well as the jargon of their profession, formed the basis for the cattle heroes of the West. The needs of cattle farmers invented the idea of wide-open spaces, shown opposite, as a prerequisite for manly endeavor.

Roundups and Trail Drives

There wasn't much need for cowboys, though, until a few enterprising Texans decided to add to their stock by rounding up all those stray, practically feral longhorn cattle, or mavericks. To do this, they enlisted just about any able-bodied man available, including Confederate vets and freed black slaves—many of whom had considerable experience working with livestock on plantations. One young cowhand, Teddy "Blue" Abbott, documented the initial roundups: "In the early days in Texas, in the '60s, when they gathered their cattle, they used to pack what they needed on a horse and go out for weeks, on a cow hunt, they called it then. That was before the name 'roundup' was invented…. The way those first trail hands were raised [was] take her as she comes and like it. They used to brag that they could go anyplace a cow could and stand anything a horse could."

The captured cattle were branded, signifying ownership; then those ready to be sold for beef were cut out of the herd. Working under the command of a trail boss, a group of cowboys herded the beef cattle, or beeves, to market in places like New Orleans, since there was more beef in Texas than there were people to eat it. A few hardy cattlemen drove their stock across the plains to California, where the Gold Rush of 1849 had significantly increased the population.

Carnivores back East clamored for beef, too, but there was no way to transport it from Texas. At that time, the railroad service ended in Missouri, and farmers there refused entry to Texas longhorns; some of them carried a tick that transmitted the fatal bovine disease Texas fever to other types of cows (though it didn't affect the beef of the longhorns, which were immune to the illness). One cattle-moving trail, known as the Goodnight-Loving Trail, went from Texas into the quarantined area; any who attempted to use it were met by groups of farmers wielding pitchforks and threatening violence.

THE CHISHOLM TRAIL

By 1867, the railroad had been extended as far as Kansas. In that year, an old wagon trail—originated by and named for the early trader Jesse Chisholm—was determined to be the most hospitable route for driving longhorns to meet the railroad in Kansas, where cattle were welcomed. The Chisholm Trail headed north from South Texas, crossed the Red River into Indian Territory (which later became the state of Oklahoma), and eventually ended a thousand miles later in the tiny frontier town of Abilene, Kansas. This town, a dusty crossroads with a few shabby businesses and lots of prairie dogs, was in the process of being converted into a cow town by an Illinois-born livestock man and entrepreneur, Joseph McCoy. After convincing the Union Pacific Railroad to build a railhead in the town, McCoy bought up 250 acres to install stockyards with pens, scales, and a barn, and began construction on a fancy hotel called the Drovers Cottage. McCoy then hired people to spread the word to cowboys that Abilene had become "a good, safe place to drive to," where a man could "ship or sell his cattle unmolested."

Beginning in the spring of 1867, the first drive from Texas, originating in San Antonio, made its way to Abilene, with twenty-four hundred head of cattle arriving there three months later. By year's end, some twenty thousand cattle had traveled east by rail, with fifteen thousand more in pens waiting for shipment or to be sold the following year. Thus began the golden age of the cowboy. It lasted about twenty-five years, as long as the cattle drive did—until the early 1890s—with a total of nine million cattle shipped to market after being driven by some forty thousand cowboys.

Jesse Chisholm (1806–1868) was a successful hunter, scout, guide, and trader. He established the cattle trail named after him almost absentmindedly. When the Civil War ended in 1865, he set off southward from near Wichita, Kansas, with a train of wagons loaded with goods for trade, following tracks left by the retreating confederate army toward Oklahoma.

Cattle drives, usually involving some two to three thousand head of cattle, consisted of ten or twelve cowhands, an older trail boss, and a cook. Texas rancher Charles Goodnight developed the strategy followed by most trail drives. In 1866 he invented the chuck wagon, an army wagon converted into a mobile kitchen and pantry with enough goods to feed the drovers (the cowboys tending the cattle) for several months on the trail. To keep the herd together and moving, a dominant steer was selected as the lead cow. One such critter, Old Blue, reportedly led ten thousand of Goodnight's cattle over several years' worth of drives.

A wrangler—normally a younger hand—took charge of the remuda, a group of fifty or so horses that traveled on the drive. Long, tedious days moving longhorns could require a cowboy to switch exhausted horses two or three times daily. In most cases, the horses belonged to the ranch, rather than to individual cowboys. Those drovers who did own a horse pooled it with the others; most cowboys treated their horses more as tools than as buddies.

With an average age of around twenty-five, cowboys came from a variety of backgrounds: Easterners seeking adventure, Texans, European immigrants, Mexicans, and ex-slaves, with roughly two-thirds being white and one-third black or Mexican. Although cowboys were ethnically diverse, racism abounded. Still, certain unwritten cowboy codes were observed: no one asked a man his last name or inquired about his past, since run-ins with the law or fighting on the wrong side of the war were not uncommon. Courage, horsemanship, stoicism, and stamina were mandatory attributes among drovers.

13

Cowpokes, as the drovers were nicknamed, chow down after a hard day in the saddle. The mobile canteen (the chuck wagon) was the preserve of the "coosie" (derived from the Spanish *cocinero*, male cook), usually an aging cowboy hired more for his wagon-handling abilities than skillet wielding. It was a sought-after position—cooks earned twice as much as cowboys because a cattle drive marches on its stomach, just as an army does.

 # RIDING THE TRAIL

The drives started in late spring or early summer, when the grasses along the way were edible and the weather had (usually) warmed up. Drovers moved the cattle from fifteen to twenty miles a day and slept out every night. It was a hard, solitary life, with only each other for company. Tricks of the trade—some rather superstitious—included placing a horsehair rope around the bedroll to protect the sleeping cowhand from a rattlesnake attack.

During grazing or watering breaks, or before turning in for the night, the cowboys would entertain themselves by playing cards, telling stories, and sometimes conducting shooting contests. Eating out of the chuck wagon, their diet consisted mainly of black coffee, beans, bacon, and biscuits. "Sonofabitch stew," first concocted by some anonymous trail cook and later becoming a cattle drive tradition, must have deserved its name:

it consisted of a cow's heart, testicles, tongue, liver, and marrow gut (the semidigested contents of the cow's gullet).

On the trail, firearms—the cowboys' gun of choice was a Colt .45—came in handy primarily for adding game to the chuck wagon's menu, killing a rattlesnake, or firing into the air to signal other drovers or to stop a stampede.

Stampedes were a hazard of the trail. Unpredictable longhorns bolted at the slightest sudden noise, from a clanging pot to a wild animal's shriek. With thousands of cattle running in a frenzy, horses and riders could be overrun, or a startled horse could throw his rider, who might then be trampled under the cattle's hooves. A cowboy could sometimes keep a stampede from progressing by firing his Colt .45 skyward in front of the lead cow.

Frederic Remington (1861–1909), the visual chronicler of the West, showed that life on the trail was not all heat and dust. The great blizzard of 1886–1887 decimated many herds on the Montana Trail. Sleepy cowhands (opposite) swap watches in the small hours. Guard was posted not just to prevent rustling but to make sure that the nervous cattle did not run amok.

The night watch had to be particularly vigilant to keep cattle from spooking. Cowhands found that singing mournful melodies could calm a restless herd. In *The Old-Time Cowhand*, Texan Ramon Adams recalls, "Away back at the beginnin' of the cow business, it didn't take the cowman long to savvy that the human voice gave cattle confidence and kept 'em from junin' 'round. I reckon it started when the herder got to hummin' a tune to keep 'imself from gettin' as lonesome as a preacher on paynight. The practice got to be so common that night herdin' was spoken of as singin' to 'em." Adams likens the sound to having "a kind of dismal heart throb like he's puttin' his mystery and misery into mournful melodies all his own."

A few famous cowboy songs originated on the trail, including "Bury Me Not on the Lone Prairie," "Whoopee Ti Yi Yo, Git Along Little Dogies," and "The Old Chisholm Trail." Teddy Blue Abbott joked about "Bury Me Not," "...they sung it to death. It was a saying on the range that even the horses nickered it and the coyotes howled it; it got so they'd throw you in the creek if you sang it. I first heard it long about '81 or '83, and by '85 it was prohibited." Musical instruments like guitars were too bulky to take on the trail; at the most, a cowhand might carry a harmonica. And campfire sing-alongs rarely occurred.

The trail end in the early years was usually a one-horse (or fewer) town, as shown in this stereopticon view. Entrepreneurs, who were quick to cash in on the cowboys' raging thirst for drink and female company, set up saloons (some of them extremely primitive) to relieve them of their temporarily fat wallets.

A Hot Time in the Old Town Tonight

The hardships, dangers, and solitude the cowboys faced for three months on the drive gave birth to their reputation as fearless, independent-minded loners. When they reached Abilene, and later other Kansas cow towns such as Wichita and, most famous of all, Dodge City, their need to blow off steam gave them their reputation as hell-raising carousers.

Off the trail, not all cowboys cut loose; some had to guard the cattle awaiting auction and rail shipment. In the early days, cowboys drove the cattle right through the streets of Abilene into the pens. Once the stock was auctioned off, cowhands prodded the cattle with poles from the pens into rail cars, earning the drovers their nicknames "cowpunchers" and "cowpokes."

Once the transaction was completed, each cowboy got paid approximately $100. Then came a bath, new clothes, and sometimes a visit to a photographer to immortalize the moment, followed by the rush to the saloon, gambling house, or brothel. As whiskey flowed, sometimes tempers flared, and occasionally gunfire rang out. Town rowdiness—usually just cowboys whooping it up— did get some local press. One Western paper reported in 1882, "Morally, as a class, they are foul-mouthed, blasphemous, drunken, lecherous, utterly corrupt, usually harmless on the plains when sober, they are dreaded in towns, for then liquor has the ascendancy over them."

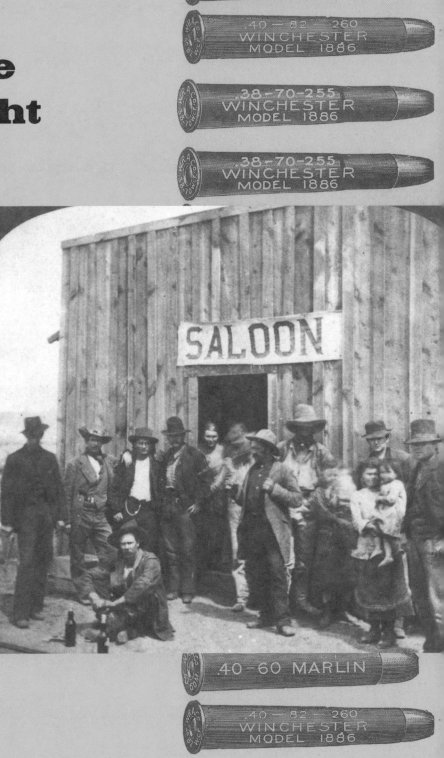

.40-60 MARLIN

.40 — 82 — 260 WINCHESTER MODEL 1886

.38-70-255 WINCHESTER MODEL 1886

.38-70-255 WINCHESTER MODEL 1886

.40-60 MARLIN

.40 — 82 — 260 WINCHESTER MODEL 1886

OUTLAWS & GUNSLINGERS

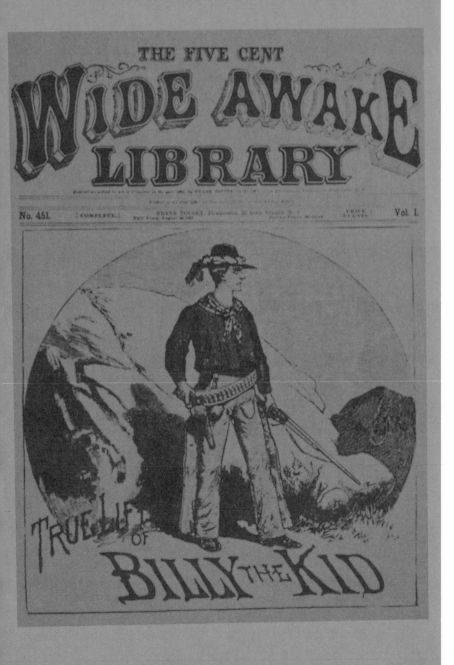

THE FIVE CENT

WIDE AWAKE LIBRARY

No. 451. | COMPLETE. | FRANK TOUSEY, Publisher, 34 Lower Street, N. Y. | PRICE 5 CENTS. | Vol. I.

TRUE LIFE OF BILLY THE KID

Much more dreaded in town, however, was a handful of outlaws and gunslingers who gave the West its "wild" reputation. Though a few of these notorious desperadoes had worked as cowboys, most had little in common with the average buckaroo. Missouri–born Jesse James and his brother Frank were Civil War vets who had ridden with Confederate terrorist gangs in Kansas led by Bloody Bill Anderson and William Quantrill. There, the brothers learned the violent tactics they would later put to use robbing banks, trains, and stagecoaches. In February 1866, the James boys led their twelve-member gang into Liberty, Missouri, and successfully carried out the first-ever daytime bank robbery. On the way out of town with about $60,000 in loot, they cold-bloodedly shot down an innocent bystander.

At large for fifteen years, the James gang devised a strategy that enabled them to successfully hold up twelve banks, seven trains, and five stagecoaches in eleven states. After carefully researching their target and wreaking havoc, the group would splinter and lay low in a network of caves and other hideouts, evading law enforcers (few in number early on), and—eventually—the Pinkerton Detective Agency, which the railroad hired. Membership in the James gang was fluid, with fellow rebel vets Cole, Jim, and Bob Younger among the most long-standing. Due to Southern loyalties, the James brothers were hailed as heroes by many locals, particularly poor rural farmers. An 1871 article in the *Kansas City Times* hailed one particularly brazen episode as "a deed so high-handed, so diabolically daring, and so utterly in contempt of fear that we are bound to admire it and revere its perpetrators."

Finally, in 1876, after a failed robbery at a bank in Northfield, Minnesota, the gang lost several members (three dead, and the three Youngers captured), and the James brothers vanished.

After living quietly (except for a handful of train robberies) under the name J. D. Howard, Jesse James was murdered in St. Joseph, Missouri, in 1882, by would-be gang member Bob Ford. Frank, under the alias B. J. Woodin, fearing for his own life, surrendered himself and his firearms shortly thereafter. Unbelievably, he was acquitted by a partial judge and jury and lived to be 72. His later sources of income included charging tourists 50 cents admission to the James family homestead. When Cole Younger got out of prison, he became a popular lecturer on the wages of sin.

No other gang achieved the long-term success and notoriety of the James gang, not even the short-lived Dalton brothers gang of Kansas who ambitiously tried robbing two banks concurrently in their hometown of Coffeyville in 1892. All three brothers and two compadres were shot down; only one brother survived and was imprisoned.

The last of the outlaw gangs was formed near the turn of the century by Utah-born Robert LeRoy Parker, who changed his name to Butch Cassidy. One member of his Hole in the Wall gang was Wyoming-native Harry Longbaugh, known as the Sundance Kid. Sundance's draw was supposedly faster than the strike of a rattlesnake. Cassidy, however, prided himself on never killing a man. Their gang of highwaymen knocked off mining camps, rustled cattle, and robbed trains, until pursuit by the Pinkertons finally splintered the gang. The likable Cassidy, with the Sundance Kid and his girlfriend Etta Place, escaped to New York in 1901, and fled from there to South America, where their crime spree continued for a decade. Though their fate is uncertain, some historians believe Cassidy and Sundance were killed by the Bolivian army.

Other charismatic, yet bloodthirsty, gunslingers led solitary lives. One of the most notorious of them was Texan John Wesley Hardin. After the Civil War, the college-educated son of a preacher began killing anyone who crossed him; over a ten-year period, he killed forty-four people. One victim was a stranger snoring too loudly in an adjacent hotel room; Hardin shot the sleeping man through the wall. Finally imprisoned for nineteen years, Hardin learned the law while doing time, became an attorney after his release in 1894, only to be murdered himself the following year by a disgruntled sheriff.

19

The short life of Billy the Kid (c. 1859–1881) has been an endlessly fascinating inspiration for dime novels (opposite), songs, and mythic biopics. His career as an outlaw only made headlines for three years, but during that time he etched himself indelibly on the American psyche. Jesse James (1847–1882) is shown above, age 17, a year after he had joined the Anderson gang. Brutalized and brutal, James was a ruthless operator, robbing banks and bullion trains with seeming impunity.

Tennessee-born Clay Allison was another loose cannon who worked as a trail hand and small-time rancher when he wasn't busy killing those who ruffled his feathers. He met his death in a wagon accident in 1887.

The most famous loner outlaw of all was Billy the Kid, born Henry McCarty in 1860 in the slums of New York City. His widowed mother took her two sons to Indiana, then New Mexico, where she died when Billy was fourteen. Calling himself William Bonney, he became a saddle tramp after a prank led to his being jailed in his hometown

of Silver City. The scrawny Kid escaped by shimmying up a chimney, then fled to Arizona. There, when he was seventeen, he killed a man for the first time after being insulted. The charismatic Bonney took off to Lincoln County, New Mexico, where he befriended a British-born cattleman named John Tunstall. Working on Tunstall's ranch, Bonney got sucked into a squabble between Tunstall and his allies and some local big shots, who bribed the law for its allegiance. After several run-ins escalated into violence, the feud became known as the Lincoln County War.

The dapper and humane Hole in the Wall gang are shown, from left to right: the Sundance Kid, Bill Carver, Ben Kilpatrick, Kid Curry, and Butch Cassidy. Sheriff Pat Garrett (opposite) brings in Billy the Kid, rather reluctantly. Garrett's role as friend and nemesis to the Kid is integral to the Billy legend.

Lincoln County War

The Tunstall side of the "war" lost. For his part in a succession of shootouts, Billy the Kid became a wanted man. He led a gang of cattle rustlers for a short time, then offered to give himself up in a deal with New Mexico Governor Lew Wallace, who double-crossed him. The Kid daringly broke out of jail every time he got caught. Still, he was constantly dogged by pursuers, led by his one-time associate, Pat Garrett. Garrett had become sheriff of Lincoln County and vowed to get the Kid. He eventually did, in July 1881, with a proverbial shot in the dark. When the twenty-one-year-old Bonney returned to spend the night at a friend's hacienda after a dance in Fort Sumner, New Mexico, Garrett came upon the unarmed Kid in a pitch-black bedroom, fired, and struck his mark.

His fame increased posthumously, after eight sensationalized "biographies" appeared, including one titled *An Authentic Life of Billy the Kid*, by Pat Garrett. Garrett wrote, "Those who knew him best will tell you in his most savage and dangerous moods his face always wore a smile." Lawman Charles Siringo, who also chased after and wrote about the Kid, concurred, calling him "a prince of a human being, who got off on the wrong foot." The Western archetype of the good bad man was born.

21

LAW ENFORCEMENT AND FAME

Garrett and Siringo were among several law enforcers who became nearly as famous as their notorious quarry. The most renowned was Illinois-born James Butler Hickok, who earned the name "Wild Bill" for having a hair-trigger temper and being as sharp with a gun as he was with cards. The former Union Army scout and superb marksman became his own best promoter, declaring to a newspaper reporter that on the Civil War battlefield he killed fifty men with fifty bullets. Wild Bill also bragged of killing a total of 100 men in the lawless West. Those who recorded his exploits seemed to revel in their descriptions of the six-foot two-inch, flamboyantly dressed, long-haired gunslinger, calling him one of the handsomest men of the West.

His notoriety as a gambler and murderer didn't keep him from being appointed marshal of Abilene in 1871 when it was in its heyday as a cow town. When John Wesley Hardin passed through, the two cordially agreed not to cross each other. Hickok remained in office until the year's end, when the town council published warnings that it would no longer tolerate "the evils of the cow business" and that drovers had to seek a new railhead for their herds. Hickok moved on, performing his marksmanship onstage, and gambling from town to town. In 1876 he landed in Deadwood, South Dakota. There, in a final poker game, he was shot in the back of the head by one Jack McCall; at that moment, Hickok was holding two aces and two eights, known forever after as the "deadman's hand."

Another gambling gunman, Wyatt Earp, with his brothers Morgan and Virgil, took over as the law in Tombstone, Arizona, a town besieged by raucous cowboys aligned with a crooked sheriff. Tombstone became legendary as the scene of the shoot-out at the O.K. Corral between the Earps, with their tubercular, alcoholic, dentist-cum-gambler pal John "Doc" Holliday, and the McLaury and Clanton brothers, cattlemen whom the Earps accused of horse theft and rustling. Bat Masterson was another renowned sharpie with cards and guns. He and his brother Ed took over the lawless cow town of Dodge City, which became more notorious than its predecessor Abilene. Both Bat and Wyatt outlived their brothers, who were eventually shot down, and survived into old age to tell tales of the Old Wild West. Earp ended his days a successful businessman in San Francisco, while Masterson became a sportswriter based in New York City. Both served as consultants to writers and filmmakers who would later chronicle those days of lawlessness. In reality, though, between them, Masterson, Earp, and Hickok killed a total of three men in the whole state of Kansas.

22

Wild Bill Hickok (1837–1876), a larger-than-life sureshooter, rode with the hares and the hounds—he was a serial lawman, inveterate gambler, and a sucker for the ladies. The end of the trail saw the cattle being herded into pens (opposite) ready for transportation by rail to the big cities back East.

BACK AT THE RANCH

Though the exploits of lawmen and outlaws got the headlines, those lifestyles were actually fairly uncommon. Among cowboys, only a small percentage died by gunfire—in Kansas, statistics show 1.5 homicides per year during the trail-driving boom of 1867–1877. Most lost their lives from stampedes or other accidents while riding the range. After spending a few days in cow towns, drovers usually headed back to the ranch. Depending on the size of the outfit, they either stayed there as a ranch hand, living in the bunkhouse, or moved on to the next job.

Most large ranches (some covered 200 square miles) employed hands to take care of raising the cattle and breaking mustangs—wild horses caught much the way mavericks were. Other chores included checking on and mending fences, another solitary pursuit called "riding fence." The month-long spring roundup required making a head count of cattle, followed by calf branding and the selection of the herd—usually four- or five-year-old cows—for the cattle drive. Some of the cattle sold in Kansas were used to start other ranches farther west, via some trail drives that took as long as six months to move the cattle to Wyoming or Montana. Eventually, by the 1880s, some 1.4 million square miles—44 percent of the country—were covered by cattle. Most of the cows grazed on open range, or free public grass, until this area became populated by homesteaders.

When the cowboys got their hard-earned down time, they occasionally competed against one another using the various skills they employed in their work: bronco-busting, roping, and hog-tying calves for branding. A similar tradition among vaqueros had taken place earlier at Mexican fiestas. Beginning in the 1860s, informal competitions took place during the end of roundup, a time celebrated by a big get-together of cowhands from several neighboring ranches. Eventually cash prizes were awarded, and as early as the 1870s, informal rodeos were being held. One nineteenth-century spectator wrote a postcard back East, raving about "Wild horses, wild cattle, wild cowboys—what a time we had!" Arguments continue over which town held the first "official" rodeo offering cash prizes; contenders include Prescott, Arizona (1888), Miles City, Montana (1891), and Cheyenne, Wyoming (1897).

The End of the Trail

Generally, cowboys worked the range for seven years before moving to town or settling down on a homestead. Through the Homestead Act of 1862, the government offered free land to farmers who "improved" it. More and more Easterners were lured west by promises of paradise from entrepreneurs and railroad promoters seeking more customers. Though the treeless, windswept plains were the opposite of Eden, many sodbusters built earthen homes and began raising sheep and a few crops. Gradually, the open range was fenced off, hastened by the introduction of barbed wire in the 1870s.

Meanwhile, the railroad continually expanded its tracks, eventually reaching into Texas, bringing to end the need for long cattle drives. Fort Worth, for example, developed into a major cow town and railhead in 1874. Ranching had become widespread in Montana and Wyoming, where railroads went too. By 1883, a handful of cattle barons owned twenty-three million cattle scattered over the West, and raising beef cattle was the region's biggest business. Representing another violent chapter in cowboy history, cattlemen became embroiled in feuds over land and rights as homesteaders gradually moved west onto the previously unoccupied range. Raising sheep or crops on lands cattlemen had used for their vast herds (each cow needed about 36 acres of grass), these homesteaders raised the ire—and violent guns—of cattlemen. Sometimes, local lawmen were paid to side with one or the other.

The final death knell for the trail drive came during the winter of 1886–1887 when a major blizzard killed millions of cattle. In 1885, Easterner-turned-rancher

25

Competitive bronco-busting began as a friendly way to celebrate the end of a long haul, but soon developed into big business, with serious bucks riding on the winner. By the twentieth century, it had become a profession in its own right. Shown opposite is Coyote Castro on Danger at the Salinas Rodeo, California, 1921. Cattle ranches in Montana, shown in the background, became increasingly more popular than the extreme Southwest as a location for big beef business.

26

Theodore Roosevelt had written, "We ourselves and the life that we lead will shortly pass away from the plains as completely as the red and white hunters who have vanished from before our herds—the broad and boundless prairies have already been bounded and...the tide of white settlement during the last few years has risen over the West like a flood and the cattlemen are...soon to be overtaken."

Little did the future president know that through his own words and example, and those of others—including his friends and colleagues Buffalo Bill Cody, Frederic Remington, and Owen Wister—the Wild West would never die, but would be immortalized as the greatest myth America has ever known. These mythmakers took the mundane reality of the cowboy and built it into a more exciting and noble lifestyle, while the exploits of notorious gunslingers became exaggerated in books, magazines, and—in the next century—moving pictures. Over the coming decades, popular culture completely transformed the hardscrabble range rider into a glamorous knight of the plains.

27

Where could the increasingly redundant cowboy turn as his natural habitat became ever more domesticated? Local rodeos (left) soaked up some of the adrenaline, but it was Buffalo Bill (William F. Cody) who realized that skills learned on the trail and the prairie could be showcased as entertainment (above).

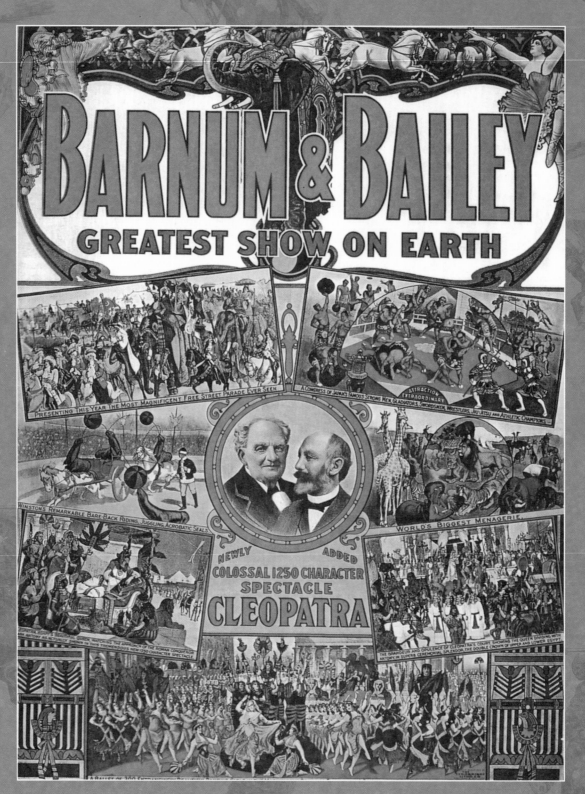

It was P.T. Barnum who said that every crowd has a silver lining, and dedicated his life to detaching it from the crowd's coat in exchange for spectacular entertainment. It was the Barnum & Bailey extravaganzas that inspired Buffalo Bill and others to create their own cowboy circuses. Charles Russell (1864–1926), self-taught cowboy artist, captured the romance of frontier life in this 1913 painting of Kit Carson and his men blazing a trail (opposite).

Whoopee Ti Yi Yo, Git Along Little Dogies

Dime Novels, Wild West Shows, "The Virginian," the Cowboy President, and Buckaroo Ballads

AS REAL COWBOY LIFE WANED IN THE WEST, SEEDS OF FANTASY REGARDING WESTERN HEROES WERE SOWN AS FAR BACK AS THE EARLY 1800S WHEN ARTISTS AND, LATER, PHOTOGRAPHERS TRAVELED WEST WITH EXPLORERS TO CAPTURE LIFE THERE.

In the beginning their subjects were Native Americans, trappers, buffalo, and landscapes. Later on, roving portrait photographers posed buckaroos in their cow-town best, holding their six-shooters and demonstrating with gestures and expressions a bravado forever associated with cowboys. Even Native Americans dressed—or were asked to dress—in warbonnets and ornate Indian "costumes" that were not actually indigenous to their particular nation. Illustrators Frederic Remington and Charlie Russell sketched and painted cowboys realistically, but in an enhanced, dramatic way. Still, these exaggerations were slight compared to the flamboyant depictions dreamed up by the authors of dime-novel fantasies.

Dime-Novel Westerns

"I might have paved for myself a far different career in letters but my early lot was cast among rough men on the border; they became my comrades."

Ned Buntline

The origins of the dime novel can be found as far back as the novels of James Fenimore Cooper. During the first half of the nineteenth century, Cooper wrote the *Leatherstocking Tales*, in which romanticized outdoorsmen faced the challenges of untamed nature and the wild frontier. Other writers quickly followed the model.

The dime novel took this idea several steps further, with lurid tales of Western adventure. These works rapidly became widespread, thanks to the invention of the rotary stream press, which allowed the quick printing on cheap paper of story after story. Patterned after England's "penny dreadfuls," these books were first created in America by Irwin and Erastus Beadle and Robert Adams in 1860. Beadle's and Adams's compact publications cost a nickel or a dime, boasted graphic covers, and were widely available during the Civil War, reportedly selling five million copies by April 1864.

Early subjects were glamorized versions of such trailblazers as Davy Crockett, Kit Carson, and Daniel Boone. In one of the Beadle novels, Carson was depicted killing seven Indians with one hand and supporting a fainting girl with the other. When Carson was shown the picture, he is said to have studied it carefully, then commented, "That there may have happened, but I ain't got no recollection of it."

The real-life characters also had imaginary counterparts, among them Seth Jones, created by Edward Ellis, one of the dime novel's earliest success stories. Based on James Fenimore Cooper's *Leatherstocking Tales*, Seth Jones benefited from an advertising campaign that roused curiosity with the question, "Who is Seth Jones?" followed by a lithograph of a coonskin-capped woodsman with the caption, "I am Seth Jones."

The James Boys and the Younger Brothers

Outlaws, lawmen, cowboys, and Indian fighters—both real and imagined—became even greater superheroes of the 1870s in titles such as *Patent Leather Joe*, or *Old Rattlesnake, the Charmer*. In their spare time around the bunkhouse, those saddle hands who were literate read dime-novel Westerns with as much eagerness as did Easterners and dudes (Easterners who moved west and dressed like cowboys), and some even tried to live up to the fantasy. Popular subjects included Billy the Kid and Jesse James, whose outlawry was frequently transformed into Robin Hood–like deeds, as well as the fictional Deadwood Dick, created by writer Edward Wheeler. After the latter's publication, the citizens of Deadwood, South Dakota, actually persuaded the town drunk to pose as Deadwood Dick for gullible tourists. Further blurring the lines between fantasy and fact, the fictional Deadwood Dick briefly married the real Calamity Jane, who fabricated her own life story.

The most famous of the dime novelists was Ned Buntline, whose life was as colorful as his writing. Known as the "world's greatest liar," Buntline (born E. Z. C. Judson) was an alcoholic who crusaded for temperance and a moralist who'd been married five times (two of the wives overlapped). He took up pulp writing, he later said, because "I might have paved for myself a far different career in letters but my early lot was cast among rough men on the border; they became my comrades, and when I made my name as a teller of stories about Indians, pirates, and scouts, it seemed too late to begin again. And besides, I made more money than any Bohemian in New York or Boston."

Reportedly hanged for shooting a man in a duel, but surviving the ordeal (other accounts had him narrowly escaping the gallows), Buntline naturally gravitated toward such larger-than-life characters as Buffalo Bill. Buntline first met the charismatic buffalo hunter, army scout, and superb storyteller in Summit Springs, Kansas, in 1869. The result was *Buffalo Bill, King of Border Men!*, originally serialized in the *New York Weekly* story paper and later transformed into several dime novels. Another pulp writer, Prentiss Ingraham, picked up the Buffalo Bill stories in 1879, making the character even more flamboyant and bloodthirsty. Between the two authors, the stage was set for the iconic William F. Cody to become America's most celebrated nineteenth-century entertainer.

31

Ned Buntline (1823–1886), shown opposite, was a dime novelist and chronic fantasist and the man who helped to make Buffalo Bill a star. His own nautical *nom de plume*—a buntline is the rope along the bottom of a square sail—dates from his four years as a midshipman (allegedly). Frank and Jesse James (seated above) are flanked by Cole and Bob Younger to form the James gang, notorious outlaws and bank robbers whose exploits were a gift to dime novelists.

BUFFALO BILL'S WILD WEST

William F. Cody was born on the frontier, in an Iowa log cabin, on February 26, 1846. By the time he was twelve, he was wielding a gun and assisting bullwhackers in their travels across the plains. His hero was frontiersman Kit Carson. As he became known for his skills on a horse and with a buffalo rifle, Cody also gained the gift of the gab. He later claimed to have been a Pony Express rider, though more likely he did short runs for the company that started the service—*after* Cody's brief tenure. As a young man, he cut a dashing figure, with long wavy hair and handsome, chiseled features. Ornate buckskins appealed to him, and floral motifs often graced his shirt or jacket front, embroidered with porcupine quills or silk. Beginning in October 1867, he earned his livelihood by hunting buffalo for the Kansas Pacific Railroad, in order to provide enough meat to feed 1,200 men. He later wrote in his autobiography,

Promotional posters for Buffalo Bill's Wild West show featured the Colonel himself, splendid in the buckskin of an army scout. He had been the Fifth Cavalry's favorite scout and won the congressional Medal of Honor in 1872 for his skill and bravery.

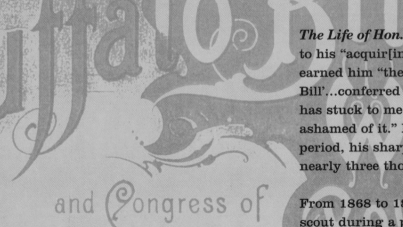

and Congress of

The Life of Hon. William F. Cody, that this led to his "acquir[ing] considerable notoriety" and earned him "the very appropriate name of 'Buffalo Bill'...conferred upon me by the road-hands. It has stuck to me ever since, and I have never been ashamed of it." Reportedly, during this eight-month period, his sharp shooting brought the bison— nearly three thousand head—closer to extinction.

From 1868 to 1876, Cody worked as an army scout during a period of uprisings by the Kiowa, Comanche, and Cheyenne. Scouts rode out ahead of the cavalry, carrying dispatches or sneaking up to spy on encamped Indians. It was dangerous work, and Cody excelled at it. He was commended for bravery when he led the Fifth Cavalry's charge against Indians, holding two women captive near Summit Springs. The action ended Indian hostilities in Kansas. It was also the occasion upon which Cody met Buntline.

Soon after publication of Buntline's embellished account of Cody's adventures, Buffalo Bill dazzled a hunting party of distinguished Easterners, including the publisher of the *New York Herald*. They invited Cody to New York, where he was given the star treatment. Coincidentally, a theatrical production based on Buntline's Cody stories was playing at the Bowery Theater. Buntline took Cody to the show and introduced him to the audience; when he ventured onto the stage, he was given a standing ovation. He turned down an offer of $500 a week to play himself in the show, declining, he later wrote, because "I never could talk to a crowd of people like that, even if it was to save my neck, and that [the director] might as well try to make an actor out of a government mule." Constant badgering by Buntline to play the lead in his new play *The Scouts of the Prairie* (reportedly written in four hours) finally convinced Cody to take to the

"BUFFALO BILL ... conferred upon me by the road-hands. It has stuck to me ever since, and I have never been ashamed of it."

William Frederick Cody (1823–1886) was the man behind the legend.

Chicago stage in 1872. Along with Buntline, Cody was accompanied by his fellow scout and buddy Texas Jack Omohundro, who soon became a dime-novel subject. Wild Bill Hickok also took part for a spell, but he shot out the stage lights a couple of times out of boredom and eventually quit and headed back West. Though panned by critics ("everything is so wonderfully bad it is almost good," crowed one), the show traveled to various cities and played to packed houses before closing in Port Jervis, New York, in 1873.

Though still an awkward amateur performer, the future showman had been bitten by the acting bug. By that time, entrepreneurs like P. T. Barnum had already fascinated Eastern audiences with traveling extravaganzas that included imported bison and a "Grand Buffalo Hunt" (in 1843!). And in 1860 mountain man Grizzly Adams had enthralled New Yorkers with his menagerie of wild animals. So in 1882, when Cody got the idea for a Wild West show to celebrate the Fourth of July in his adopted hometown of North Platte, Nebraska, the concept wasn't entirely new. He advertised for cowboys to take part in riding, roping, and shooting competitions at "The Old Glory Blowout"; one thousand showed up. His own demonstration of buffalo hunting thrilled audiences. The next year an inspired Cody, in cahoots with fellow entrepreneur Doc Carver, launched the Rocky Mountain and Prairie Exhibition in Omaha, Nebraska. Among the attractions were a Pony Express reenactment, a simulated attack on the Deadwood Treasure Wagon, a bareback pony race, roping and riding buffalo, and the "Grand Hunt on the Plains," climaxing in a battle between Indians and the cavalry.

In 1884 Carver left to start his own show, and Cody's eventually became known as Buffalo Bill's Wild West Show and Congress of Rough Riders of the World.

The Wild West Show was larger than life, staged with a huge cast of humans and animals. It toured America and Europe. Here it is at the Olympia exhibition theater in London, where it was seen by Queen Victoria.

A BRONCHO BUSTER   CHIEF EAGLE SHIRT

36

The three-hour outdoor extravaganza had a tremendous effect on America's notions of cowboys and the Wild West. The reality of taming the frontier, which could be backbreaking and mundane as well as violent and exciting, was romanticized by Cody to the extent that, according to historian Sarah Blackstone, "the truth was so totally mixed with the myth as to be indistinguishable." Buffalo Bill hired Buck Taylor, who'd participated in trail drives and worked at Cody's ranch, and crowned him King of the Cowboys. Soon, Taylor's exploits on the range were fodder for Prentiss Ingraham's dime novels. Young Johnny Baker became the "Cowboy Kid." By 1885, Cody had enlisted his biggest headliners, Annie "Miss Sureshot" Oakley and Sitting Bull, the legendary chief who defeated Custer. Oakley's act included shooting the ashes off the cigarette in her husband Frank Butler's mouth, and firing at an apple on her poodle's head. Sitting Bull was the only one to insist on a written contract; this gave the shrewd negotiator all the money netted from sales of his autograph and photograph—as well as fresh oysters on demand.

Buffalo Bill took the Wild West to Europe for the first time in 1887, even performing before its crowned heads, Queen Victoria included, who wrote that "cowboys were fine-looking people." In Rome, Buffalo Bill hoped to set up at the ruins of the Coliseum—but the space wasn't large enough!

The show did a six-month stint in Paris, where its vendors introduced popcorn to the French. As the show traveled America and Europe, the idea of the Wild West became that of this consummate showman, whose own authentic experiences had blurred with the fantastic, perhaps even in his own mind.

Many other touring Wild West shows emerged, including those run by Doc Carver, Gordon "Pawnee Bill" Lillie, and Jack "the Poet Scout" Crawford, who had all at one time participated in Buffalo Bill's outfit. By the turn of the century, there were an estimated eighty touring companies of Wild West shows. Even former outlaws Cole Younger and Frank James teamed up to form a short-lived traveling show.

A poster for the Miller Bros. 101 Ranch show (above, top) promotes the entertainment's authenticity. When the motion pictures turned their glare on the West, it was Miller Bros. 101 that supplied the stuntworkers, extras, and Indian war bands. Buck Taylor, shown above, center, was the first King of the Cowboys (Roy Rogers would later inherit the crown). Taylor was one of the stars of the Wild West show. Little Annie Oakley (opposite), Buffalo Bill's female lead, proves that you can indeed get a man with a gun.

Wild West shows retained their popularity into the twentieth century, with newly christened cowboy stars forming their own extravaganzas into the 1950s. One of the most influential and long-running shows was the Miller Bros. 101 Ranch and Real Wild West, which evolved from a large cattle ranch in Bliss, Oklahoma, spawning several of the twentieth century's flamboyant new cowboy stars. It prided itself on its authenticity as a real working ranch, and made much of the fact in its 1912 souvenir program: "The Real Thing: We come straight from the Land of Cattle, Cabins, Cowboys, and Cow Trails. That is our authority and license for a Real 'Wild West' Show and its Guarantee of being an Original, Genuine, Authentic, Out-and-Out Honest, Real Exposition of Western Frontier Life and History, without recourse to Circus Tanbark, Vaudeville, Theatrics, or Disguise. Our Brand stands for Stern Honesty wherever it is stamped.... The real life of ranch, range, roundup, and Indian camp will be reproduced in all its vivid and romantic picturesqueness by actual, living figures of the frontier.... The 101 Ranch has remained intact in all its vastness despite the influx of the small farmer into Oklahoma...."

By 1916, Buffalo Bill himself would join the Miller Bros. 101 Ranch show. Just as he'd been no stage actor, Buffalo Bill was no businessman either. His show earned him some $1 million in 1893, the year it appeared at the Great Columbia Exposition, or Chicago World's Fair, yet Cody eventually went bankrupt after several bad business dealings. Even though his Wild West show was dissolved, the dramatization and glamorization of the West were confirmed and were taking new forms.

From his years as a scout, Buffalo Bill had forged friendships with various Indian nations and their leaders. Sitting Bull (Tatanka-Iyotanka), chief of Hunkpapa Lakota, joined the Wild West show for four months in 1885; he rode once around the arena every performance for $50 a week. Frederic Remington's hard-riding old cowhand (opposite), painted in 1902, is an idealization of a life long past.

THE WILD WEST IN PICTURES

By the 1880s, national magazines such as *Harper's Weekly* were commissioning writers and artists to cover the West for their readers—readers who much preferred fiction over fact. New York–born artist Frederic Remington ventured west and began creating a number of realistic yet romanticized drawings of cowboys to illustrate articles describing their adventures. In the 1890s

Remington turned to clay and bronze to create his heroic cowboys, beginning with the 1895 sculpture *The Bronco Buster*.

In 1881, as a teenager obsessed with the Wild West, Charlie Russell moved from St. Louis to a Montana ranch and completely transformed into a range-riding buckaroo. The self-taught artist worked on numerous cattle drives, sketching and painting in his spare time. Russell sometimes traded his art for a glass of whiskey or a plate of food before eventually getting magazine commissions and selling his work to collectors. He had lived the life he painted, and felt no qualms about depicting it as dramatically as possible.

39

THE VIRGINIAN

WESTERNS HAVE FUNCTIONED AS MORALITY PLAYS OF GOOD IN CONFLICT WITH EVIL

William Bloodworth

Another young man who fell in love with the West was Owen Wister, a Harvard law student who traveled to Wyoming for his health. Wister was born in Germantown, Pennsylvania, in 1860, the year that also saw the birth of the dime novel. He would create the character that has most influenced the world's idea of the cowboy in his novel *The Virginian*. Raised in Philadelphia, the son of a country doctor and a mother who translated French poetry and wrote for the *Atlantic Monthly*, Wister initially pursued a career in music, which he studied at Harvard. There he met fellow student Teddy Roosevelt. After graduation in 1882, Wister traveled in Europe, followed by a trip west at twenty-four. From a ranch in Buffalo, Wyoming, he wrote home, "Yesterday I got on a bronco for the first time. Had a roundup yesterday and cut out the black cattle."

Wister returned East to attend law school and became an attorney, but, as he later related, he "couldn't get Wyoming out of my head." At the suggestion of a friend, he began writing about the "heroes of the sagebrush," and had his first cowboy story published in *Harper's* magazine. He gave up law, traveled west again, and penned more stories, which were collected in *Red Men and White* (1896). Two novels followed; then, in April 1902, the publication of *The Virginian: Horseman of the Plains*, a portrait of a gallant yet sensitive Western loner who followed his own strict code of honor. This cowboy archetype contrasted greatly with the brash, gun-waving figures of the dime novels. Wister's noble protagonist, a somewhat genteel Southerner known only as "the Virginian," transformed the idea of a cowboy into an individualist who never strayed from his Western code, no matter the cost. Though he'd sooner get by on his wits, the Virginian uses violence when necessary. He participates in frontier justice in the Wyoming territory, resulting in the lynching of rustlers, and faces the range bully Trampas in a shoot-out, risking his relationship with the pacifist Vermont-born schoolmarm, Molly Wood. In the end, of course, she sticks by the Virginian. "Ever since *The Virginian*," according to Western literature scholar William Bloodworth, "Westerns have functioned as morality plays of good in conflict with evil, with the results portrayed in such a way as to idealize the past in contrast to the present." The novel became an instant success, translated into several languages, and Wister himself adapted it into

Gentlemanly Gary Cooper (left) played the Virginian to perfection in Victor Fleming's 1929 movie. Wister (opposite) dedicated his creation to future president Teddy Roosevelt, another Harvard dude who transformed himself into a cowboy. The cover of the first edition of Wister's seminal novel is shown in an inset; the story would go on to form the basis of four movies and two TV series.

a popular stage production. Much later, there were to be film and television versions.

Nostalgia for the waning of the West, a sentiment expressed in Wister's preface, surely had a lot to do with the enduring success of both his book and play. "What is become of the horseman, the cowpuncher, the last romantic figure upon our soil?" Wister wrote. "For he was romantic. Whatever he did, he did with his might...he will be here among us always, invisible, waiting his chance to live and play as he would like. His wild kind has been among us always, since the beginning: a young man with his temptations, a hero without wings."

41

THE VIRGINIAN

R   R

OWEN·WISTER

Rough Riders

W ister, who never wrote another Western novel, dedicated *The Virginian* to his college friend Theodore Roosevelt, the other man most responsible for America's love affair with the West. The myopic and asthmatic New York State assemblyman first ventured west in 1883. After his wife and mother died in February of the following year, he moved to a ranch in the Dakota territory. He outfitted himself with buckskins and firearms, bought large herds of cattle, and practically willed himself into becoming a cowboy. The New York "dude" proved a good shot and an able range rider, and eventually won the trust of dubious cowhands. Roosevelt saw a pure American character in the cowboy and carried that image with him for the rest of his life. In his 1896 book *Ranch Life and the Hunting Trail* (illustrated by Frederic Remington), he glowingly described range riders as "hardy and self-reliant as any men who ever breathed—with bronzed, set faces and keen eyes that look all the world in the face without flinching…. Except while on…sprees they are quiet, rather self-contained men, perfectly frank and simple…. There is a high regard for truthfulness and keeping one's word, intense contempt for any kind of hypocrisy, and a hearty dislike of a man who shirks his work…. He possesses, in fact, few of the emasculated, milk-and-water moralities admired by pseudo-philanthropists, but he does possess, to a very high degree, the stern, manly qualities that are invaluable to a nation."

Roosevelt eventually returned East to continue his political career. In 1898, inspired by Buffalo Bill's Wild West and Congress of Rough Riders of the World, he organized his own Rough Riders to fight on horseback in the Spanish–American War; he returned a hero from battle in Cuba. In 1900, he became William McKinley's vice president; when McKinley was assassinated the following year, "the cowboy president" took office, winning reelection in 1904.

42

"hardy and self-reliant as any men who ever breathed"

Roosevelt's Rough Riders (above and opposite), inspired by Buffalo Bill's Wild West show, took the cowboy myth and ethos and made it work back in the real world.

Another dude whose life changed owing to his infatuation with the West was an Ohio-born dentist-turned-writer named Zane Grey. After taking a trip in 1907 to Arizona soon after reading *The Virginian*, the novelist focused his imagination on cowboys. In 1910 he wrote the first of a long line of best-sellers filled with buckaroos and Western events, including *Riders of the Purple Sage* (1913), which sold over a million copies. His work was so popular it was made into more than 130 movies over the coming decades.

NO DISCOURAGING WORDS

As books, magazines, and plays about the cowboy became popular, so did songs written about buckaroos riding the range begin showing up in living rooms and parlors via songbook folios. The song "Whoopee Ti Yi Yo, Git Along Little Dogies" was first mentioned in the 1903 book *Log of a Cowboy*, by drover Andy Adams. In 1908, Jack Thorp privately published a collection titled *Songs of the Cowboy*; two years on, Texas-born folklorist John Lomax issued his first gathering of folk songs, *Cowboy Songs and other Frontier Ballads*. Lomax grew up on a farm near the Chisholm Trail and began collecting songs from cowhands as a teen. Soon, Americans in all parts of the country knew the words to "Whoopee Ti Yi Yo, Git Along Little Dogies," "Home on the Range," and "Bury Me Not on the Lone Prairie." To meet the public demand, Tin Pan Alley tunesmiths who'd never ventured west in their lives began penning cowboy numbers, beginning in 1905 with "Cheyenne (Shy Anne)," followed a few years later by "Ragtime Cowboy Joe." "Numerous songs added to the cowboy's appeal as a colorful, rugged individual," points out Western culture scholar Richard Aquila, "an American knight astride his trusty steed jousting against the twin perils of the Wild West and civilization."

Taking up where dime novels, Buffalo Bill, *The Virginian*, and cowboy songs left off, a newly developed form of entertainment— moving pictures—was beginning to blur even further the lines between the fantasy and reality of cowboy life. By the end of the first decade of the twentieth century, it was no longer possible to tell the real West from that of the imagination.

This iconic shot is from the first full-fledged Western, *The Great Train Robbery* (1903), directed by Edwin S. Porter.

The dapper D. W. Griffith (extreme left in the background photo opposite) is shown on the set of *The Battle of Elderbush Gulch* (1913), one of the last Westerns he made for the Biograph film company.

How the Western Was Born
"The Great Train Robbery," Broncho Billy, and Early Movie Milestones

WITH THE COMING OF MOTION PICTURES, THE COWBOY WAS BROUGHT INTO THE LIVES OF NEARLY EVERY AMERICAN. BEGINNING IN THE 1890S WITH DOCUMENTARY-STYLE GLIMPSES OF BRONCO BUSTERS AT WORK AND BUFFALO BILL'S WILD WEST, THE "FLICKERS" DEPICTED THE EXCITEMENT OF COW COUNTRY.

When melodrama and action were added to the equation, a new art form—the Western—was born. The Western would not simply preserve the West, but prolong its natural life.

It seems fitting somehow that Buffalo Bill "starred" in one of the very earliest moving pictures. Thomas Edison's invention was put to work in 1894 in order to document the Buffalo Bill Wild West Show and Congress of Rough Riders. Flickering images show the handsome, long-haired, bearded Cody putting his horse Isham through his paces, surrounded by buckaroos twirling lassos. "Actuality films" depicting roundups, Native American scenes, calf branding, and grazing buffalo herds were soon joined by staged events such as stagecoach holdups, but with no real plots or acting.

In 1898 the Edison Company for the first time filmed little vignettes that told a story of sorts. *Poker at Dawson City* presented a table of cardplayers who begin cheating and get into a brawl. With a slightly more developed story line, *Cripple Creek Bar-room* featured a rustic saloon filled with unsavory-looking cowpokes and a top-hatted big shot. Drunkenness ensues and the intoxicated patrons get the heave-ho. A short historical vignette, *Kit Carson*, was released by the American Mutoscope and Biograph Company in September, 1903.

Two months on, the Edison Company performed a cinematic leap. Most film historians consider *The Great Train Robbery*, directed by Edwin S. Porter, to be the first narrative Western of consequence. It was supposedly inspired by a real train robbery that took place in 1900. Creatively photographed and edited, the ten-minute movie established an early formula for Westerns. It included a dramatic train robbery—filmed near Dover, New Jersey, on the Delaware and Lackawanna Railroad—followed by an exciting escape through woods with guns a-smokin'. Another scene that became standard was a saloon confrontation where a dude is forced to dance by a desperado shooting at his feet. *Train Robbery* also had one of the first powerful close-ups— a black-hatted, mustachioed bad guy firing his six-shooter into the camera lens, straight at the viewer.

Audiences flocked to see *Train Robbery*. For a few cents more, they could even watch a hand-tinted "color" version. Its success initiated another cinematic trend—imitation. Other companies came up with their own versions of the film, including *The Holdup of the Rocky Mountain Express*, *The Great Bank Robbery*, and *The Bold Bank Robbery*. The Lubin Company of Philadelphia actually remade the movie frame by frame, the only difference being the calendar page on the station wall. Edison retaliated with a parody, *The Little Train Robbery*.

A Chicago company, Selig-Polyscope, was the first to send a troupe out west to film, resulting in *The Girl from Montana* and *Western Justice* (1907). It was praised by an early trade journal for its "marvelously stirring and sensational chase." Meanwhile, the Eastern Westerns, with their painted backdrops and homemade cowboy outfits, were sometimes so obviously bogus that Western movie houses refused to show them. By 1908, both Selig and the Essanay Company had set up operations in Colorado.

A bullet ballet is a lasting memory from the seminal *The Great Train Robbery*. Although only ten minutes long, and now a museum piece, Porter's pioneering film was packed with incident and established some of the ground rules of the Western genre.

BRONCHO BILLY AND THE FOOTLOOSE BUCKAROO

Essanay was formed in 1907 by George Spoor and Gilbert M. Anderson—hence the name. Anderson, born Max Aronson in New York, had gotten his feet wet as an actor on *The Great Train Robbery*. Trying out as an outlaw, he fell off his horse and was demoted to bit parts. He later moved to Vitagraph, where he first acted then began directing. After forming Essanay, the stocky Anderson took over the studio's production in

Colorado before moving the company to Niles, California. In 1910, when he couldn't find an actor suitable for the role, he took the lead in Essanay's one-reeler *Broncho Billy's Redemption*. Here was another landmark. For the first time, a Western was focused around a central character, this one based on a melodramatic story by Peter B. Kyne called "Broncho Billy and the Baby." Though not much of a looker, Anderson had a likable quality and was

49

quite compelling in his role as an outlaw softened by the love of a woman and her baby. Audiences ate it up, and so began a string of super-successful Broncho Billy pictures. Anderson and Broncho Billy became one and the same in his public's adoring consciousness. Usually two reels long (each reel lasting about ten minutes), the Broncho Billy Westerns had strong plots for the day, establishing the structure and character types upon which an entire genre would be based. The first cowboy star eventually played the lead in three hundred or so films, resulting in the footloose buckaroo role becoming the most prominent one of the early Westerns.

Meantime, other movie companies had been experimenting with shooting pictures on location in the West. In 1908 the Oklahoma Mutoscene Company made *The Bank Robbery* with "director" William Tilghman, a famous lawman who'd been marshal of Dodge City from 1884–86. Tilghman hired train robber Al Jennings, who'd just been released from prison, to play one of the robbers. Tilghman didn't turn out to be much of a director, but Jennings went on to star in numerous two-reelers, including *The Fugitive's Life* and *The*

Tryout. His notoriety made this possible, no doubt, judging from one film historian's description of him: "As a Western hero, Al violated every precept in the book. Short and thin, almost anemic in appearance, his craggy face lined by 46 years and accentuated by a shock of unruly auburn hair, he could only be described as a homely professional ex-bandit playacting for the camera." Indeed, Jennings won parts due to his credentials as a real outlaw, but the more realistic he tried to make his character, the less well-received his films became. Audiences wanted him to look the part of the buckaroo whose image had been forged by Wild West shows, dime novels, and Remington and Russell paintings. Wyatt Earp actually appeared in one film but, according to the director, "could not act convincingly enough to perform regularly in pictures."

As more and more flickers were shot in Texas, Oklahoma, Colorado, and California, unemployed range riders, reservation Indians, and other former outlaws such as Henry Starr and Emmett Dalton joined up, just as some had earlier found work in Wild West shows. If their appearance didn't fit the bill, they were dressed in costumes to make them appear "more realistic."

Broncho Billy, shown opposite, is the first reel hero, who went on to star in some three hundred adventures. The townsfolk confront the sheriff in the still above in a typical two-reeler from Spoor and Anderson's eponymous Essanay company. A washout on the silver screen, Wyatt Earp (background photo) found his temperament better suited to business and consultancy after retiring from his epic career as lawman.

"...the Bison Company's Indians are always
splendid fellows to behold..."

THOMAS INCE & D. W. GRIFFITH

In 1910 the Bison Movie Company moved from the East to the Santa Ynez Canyon, near Santa Monica, California, where it leased 18,000 acres. By chance, the Miller Bros. 101 Ranch Wild West happened to be touring in the area. The two outfits struck a deal: the Oklahoma ranch's huge holdings of Western accoutrements, including stagecoaches, tepees, herds of buffalo and cattle, and authentic cowboys and Native Americans, would settle down on the Bison acreage. The renamed company, Bison 101, began making large-scale Westerns, directed by Thomas Ince.

A former actor himself, Ince had worked as a director in New York and Cuba. Rather than an artistic visionary behind the camera, Ince was more of a producer. He organized his Westerns down to every minute item, coming up with detailed shooting scripts that would become the industry standard. Soon the California ranch was known as Inceville, and its films were receiving notices such as "the Bison Company's Indians are always splendid fellows to behold and, what is more, they always look what they are supposed to be." The company's forte was drawing upon historical events and showing complex plots dealing with issues of ethnic diversity, such as the consequences of white settlers invading Native American lands. As in *War on the Plains* (1912), plots of the one- or two-reel films usually climaxed around battles between cowboys or cavalry and Indians. Ince's well-crafted *The Indian Massacre* presented both sides of the story, depicting the settlers and cowboys as brave, but also showing the injustices inflicted upon Native Americans. "Its closing scene—a silhouette of an Indian woman praying beneath the wood-frame burial pyre of her dead child—was as beautifully composed and photographed as anything in later John Ford films," according to Western film historian William Everson. Eventually Bison 101 was absorbed into another company, Universal, which would become the largest producer of Westerns through the 1920s.

Another East-coast director schlepped his crew to California beginning in the winter of 1910 to take advantage of the better light and escape the bad weather. David Wark—D. W.—Griffith worked for the Biograph Company, first as a writer/actor, then as a director. Kentucky-born Griffith started as an actor in 1907 in the Edison film *Rescued from an Eagle's Nest*, directed by Edwin S. Porter. Between 1908 and 1913, Biograph created seventy-four Westerns, with Griffith's sophisticated direction and dramatic verve giving the genre astonishing new possibilities. Griffith's films were large-scale spectacles, mostly filmed in the West, like the Ince pictures. His films

Thomas Ince (following the action, above, and surrounded by his Bison Company Indians, opposite) brought gravitas and spectacle to the genre, and his movies acknowledged the presence and plight of Native Americans.

also benefited from Griffith's imaginative camera work, particularly his innovative crosscutting, and the engaging performances he drew from such actors as Lillian Gish and Mae Marsh, who starred in his elaborate 1913 Western *The Battle of Elderbush Gulch*. Other classic Griffith Westerns include *The Last Drop of Water* (1911) and *Fighting Blood*, both of which, in just a couple of reels, managed to captivate audiences with their drama and tension. Griffith created by far the most compelling cliff-hangers of the day.

Like Broncho Billy, both Ince and Griffith made little morality plays with their movies; for Ince the clear-cut struggle between good and evil was represented by good being associated with the church and evil with the saloon. Alcohol also caused the downfall of the "bad guy" in Griffith films, such as *Last Drop of Water*. Ince and Griffith both accentuated the realism of the locations of their films, making the dusty West come alive on the screen.

MGM-997

New Developments

Of course, the most famous "location" for America's filmmaking industry is Hollywood. But the movies did not come to Hollywood until 1913—and then it was almost by accident. Cecil B. DeMille, a protégé of Griffith's, wanted to shoot *The Squaw Man* in Flagstaff, Arizona, but a snowstorm meant a change of plan. Instead, he took the production to Hollywood, where the Nestor company had recently built a studio. Starring a popular actor named Dustin Farnum, the film had been a stage play and told the story of a white man who marries an Indian woman. It became the first movie made in Hollywood.

Another new development in filmmaking was the serial. The earliest, *What Happened to Mary?* (1913) was made by the Edison Company to tie in with a newspaper serial. The following year *The Hazards of Helen* featured some Western elements, in that the heroine was constantly being tied to a train track by the villain. The first truly episodic Western was *Liberty*, made in 1916. This twenty-episode serial was produced by Universal and starred Jack Holt, who played in many Westerns. All told, sixty Western serials were made during the silent era, the most famous being *Winners of the West*, the first of the historical Western serials.

53

Lillian Gish (opposite), who had seen great success in D. W. Griffith's early films, continued to bring a feminine presence to an otherwise rugged canon. Here she is in Victor C. Seastrom's *The Wind* (1928), a melodrama of love and death set on the Texas plains, in what many believe was Gish's finest performance. Epicmeister Cecil B. DeMille (above), directing *The Squaw Man*, an exploration of racism against Native Americans.

REALITY VERSUS FANTASY

In the first years of filmmaking, Broncho Billy was the only cowboy star to play solely in Westerns. Douglas Fairbanks had had the lead role in several early ones, but between other films. Most leading actors lacked the necessary skills to play believable buckaroos. Some could barely throw a punch with vigor, much less fall off a horse, or lasso a steer. That's where real cowboys (and some girls) came in. They were hired as the first stuntmen, often doubling for the lead. The most famous, Yakima Canutt, was a champion rodeo rider when he began working in movies in 1917. He devised some of the earliest tricks to make violent escapades look real, without anyone getting hurt—most of the time.

By the mid-teens, Westerns were an established and important genre of American filmmaking. As more studios, directors, actors, and stuntmen cut their teeth on these films, a few authentic Westerners fell by the wayside when they tried the same. The nephew of notorious female outlaw Belle Starr, Henry (also a desperado), bought an interest in the Pan American Motion Picture company when he got out of prison in 1919. That year he

starred in *A Debt to the Law*, a reenactment of the double bank robbery attempted by the Dalton gang in 1892. The movie was a success, but Starr was cheated out of his earnings by his partner. He hired a team of lawyers to retrieve his money, but lost the case. What

could he do? He robbed a bank, and was shot dead by a teller.

That greatest showman of the nineteenth century, Buffalo Bill, decided to get into the picture business too, years after he'd starred in the actuality films. In September 1913, and in financial difficulties, he joined a partnership to form the Colonel W. F. Cody

(Buffalo Bill) Historical Pictures Company, financed by the Essanay company. Cody no longer had his huge array of Western props and equipment; it had been sold when he declared bankruptcy. His large company of cowboys, Indians, and rough riders had all moved on to other Wild West shows or retired. But with his extensive contacts, Cody was able to pull enough strings to persuade the U.S. Secretary of War and the U.S. Secretary of the Interior to allow his company to "borrow" three troops of U.S. Cavalry for filming.

How was Buffalo Bill's movie? We'll never know. The film was lost and no copies have ever been found. Apparently, though, Cody didn't find the final result very gratifying and declared that filmmaking was "harder than three circuses in one." It was Buffalo Bill's first and only venture into motion-picture making. Four years on, in 1917, he died a broken man. But of course, his flickering image does live on—not only in those early Edison films, but in dozens of motion pictures made decade after decade with the most famous movie stars of the day playing their own interpretation of the King of the Bordermen.

Henry Starr (above) was a real-life desperado who was outsmarted by the movie business and went back to doing what he did best. After a lifetime of showmanship, Buffalo Bill, seen opposite with partner Pawnee Bill (G. W. Lillie), made his last stand behind the lens in a project that was bankrolled by ardent fan Broncho Billy Anderson at the Essanay company. Cody received $50,000 for his participation.

WILLIAM FOX PRESENTS

Buck Jones
in
HEARTS AND SPURS

Based on the Thrilling story 'THE OUTLAW'
BY JACKSON GREGORY · SCENARIO BY JOHN STONE
DIRECTED BY W. S. VAN DYKE

CARL LAEMMLE presents

HOOT GIBSON
in
"The SADDLE HAWK"

WITH MARION NIXON · G. RAYMOND NYE · JOSIE SEDGWICK · FRANK CAMPEAU
DIRECTED BY EDWARD SEDGWICK

UNIVERSAL GIBSON PRODUCTION

HIS WAY THROUGH
DANGER
FOR LOVE
and HONOR!

TIM McCOY
in

WILLIAM FOX presents

Tom Mix
with TONY, the Wonder Horse
in
The GREAT K&A Train Robbery

The Foremost Western Thriller of the Greatest Western Star
from PAUL LEICESTER FORD'S novel · Scenario by JOHN STONE

LEW SEILER PRODUCTION

S·A·LYNCH ENTERPRISES, INC.
PRESENT

WM·S·HART
in
THE COLD DECK

A SUPERLATIVE PRODUCTION

CARL LAEMMLE
OFFERS

HARRY CAREY
IN THE FIRST WESTERN SUPER PRODUCTION EVER MADE
THE FOX
DIRECTED BY ROBERT THORNBY

UNIVERSAL-JEWEL MASTERPIECE

A Western Masquerade
William S. Hart, Tom Mix, and Other Silent Cowboy Stars

BRONCHO BILLY PICTURES WHETTED AUDIENCES' APPETITES FOR SOMETHING NEW: COWBOY MOVIE STARS. IN THE SILENT ERA, SEVERAL MAJOR CELLULOID COWBOYS CAME TO THE SCREEN.

The new cowboy movie stars—William S. Hart, Tom Mix, Fred Thomson, Harry Carey, Tim McCoy, Hoot Gibson, Buck Jones, and Ken Maynard—brought with them a distinctive style that attracted legions of fans. But by 1911, some critics—such as those at the trade journal *Nickelodeon*—were describing the Western genre as "a gold mine that had been worked to the limit." To the rescue charged William Surrey Hart.

WILLIAM S. HART

Born in Newburgh, New York, in 1864, Hart spent some time in the West as a child. A few encounters with cowhands and Native Americans made a lasting impression on him. As a young man in New York, Hart became a stage actor, cutting his teeth on Shakespeare. His first major role came in an 1889 production of *Ben Hur*; the play was based on the book written by New Mexico Governor Lew

Wallace, who'd double-crossed Billy the Kid in 1879. In 1905, Hart was cast in his first Westerner role, playing on Broadway in the melodrama *The Squaw Man*; his character, Cash Hawkins, marries an Indian woman and has to deal with the consequences of racism. Hart then won the lead in *The Virginian*, the adaptation of Owen Wister's book. On tour in the Midwest, Hart saw some cowboy flickers in his spare time. Appalled by the inaccurate portrayals of the West he'd experienced in his youth, he vowed to make realistic Westerns.

After a couple of movie roles as the villain, Hart looked up an old friend and former roommate, Thomas Ince. At this point, Ince was looking to make other types of films. He told Hart that Westerns were finished because the market was flooded: "They are the cheapest pictures to make," Hart later recalled Ince saying, "and every company out here has made them. You simply cannot sell a Western picture at any price. They are a drug on the market." The forty-six-year-old Hart convinced him to give it a try. Under contract for $125 a week, Hart made his first motion picture, *The Bargain* (1914), which he cowrote; it was followed by *On the Night Stage*.

Hart's movies combined vivid storytelling, sentiment, action, and a degree of historical accuracy—plus his own rugged good looks and strong performances. They quickly became popular with audiences. As a result, Hart gained the clout to control his projects creatively, eventually directing most of his pictures. He tried to convey on-screen the truth and poetry of the authentic, historical West, while imbuing each role with his own personal charisma. At six foot two, lean and lanky, with a long face, Hart transformed himself from Eastern Shakespearian thespian into scruffy, austere Western range rider. He took his cowboy role seriously, seeking out the real veterans of the Wild West as consultants, including Bat Masterson and Wyatt Earp. He first met Masterson while he was performing in *The Squaw Man,* when the former lawman wrote him a note commending him on his "exceptionally good" portrayal of a "cowboy desperado." The action in

58

Strong and silent, the early cowboy stars were so popular that they usually had bigger billing than the movie titles (previous page, left). William S. Hart (in costume), the original enigmatic lone cowboy, discusses technical points with his director (previous page, right). A late starter on the silver screen, Hart did not take up six-gun and spurs until he was 49, then crammed 65 movies into an 11-year career.

Hart's movies took place in authentic-looking ramshackle, dusty Western towns, giving the films a raw, unglamorous look.

Hart was the first screen cowboy to put his horse in the spotlight, appearing with his pinto pony Fritz in every outing. In his characters, Hart continued the "good badman" tradition pioneered by Broncho Billy. Setting a pattern for decades of Westerns to come, Hart's characters were often loners who set out to rescue a corrupt town overrun by bad guys. A typical Hart role was his heathen bartender reformed by a preacher's daughter in 1915's *Every Inch a Man*. In another of his best films, 1916's apocalyptic *Hell's Hinges*, Hart's dastardly outlaw is transformed by his love for a lovely, spiritually inclined damsel, with his subtitle declaring, "I reckon God ain't wantin' me much, ma'am, but when I look at you I feel I've been ridin' the wrong trail." Brashly sentimental, Hart's films depicted his own idealized theories of the redemptive qualities and possibilities of the West and its denizens. They also revived the Western's popularity and influenced other actors and filmmakers.

HARRY CAREY

Harry Carey, though nowhere nearly as big a star as Hart, was his closest contemporary in terms of style. Also a New York-born stage actor, Carey began in motion pictures in 1910 and learned to ride horses well enough to make Westerns. Carey's approach, like Hart's, was to play a more realistic cowpuncher, whose code of honor forced him to commit violent acts if necessary. One of his characters was Cheyenne Kincaid, dressed in black and wielding a whip. Craggy-faced and older, Carey projected an earnest authenticity that found favor among directors and influenced several future cowboy stars.

Cecil B. DeMille (opposite) is shown on the set of his second version of *The Squaw Man* with leading lady Lupe Velez (Naturich, the "squaw"). DeMille's first take on the drama was during the silent era, with Charles Bickford playing the lead. Harry Carey (right) is shown in *Tiger Thompson* (1924), which also had a role for his three-year old son, Harry Jr.

By 1920, Hart's place as preeminent purveyor of the West on-screen had been usurped by a stunning daredevil who had started out in cheapo Westerns made by the Selig Company. Showman Tom Mix brought a flamboyant on-screen style to the celluloid cowboy, along with a fantasy depiction of buckaroos as clean-cut superheroes who always prevailed. In contrast to Hart's grimy realism and moralistic messages, Mix's cartoonish approach offered thrills-and-chills entertainment, pure and simple. His sharpshooting, fast-riding, hard-hitting cowboy won every fight and escaped from every trap, establishing a flashy new archetype for the Western hero. Mix, like Hart before him, inspired many imitators. Though the two actors had very different styles, they set the mold for the two major types of cowboy character to follow over the next four decades.

Born in 1880 in Mix Run, Pennsylvania, Mix was one of the first major film stars to have experience as a buckaroo before making a career in the movies. He polished his roping and riding skills working at a Western dude ranch, then performed with Colonel Zack Mulhall's Wild West Show. This was followed in 1906 by a stint with the prestigious Miller Bros. 101 Ranch and Wild West Show, where he earned the title World Champion Cowboy in 1908. Mix claimed to have served heroically in the Spanish–American War as a Rough Rider, but records don't bear this out. He broke into the movie business in 1909 when William Selig's Polyscope Movie Company used his ranch as the location for the pseudo-documentary *Ranch Life in the Great South West*. Originally hired to supervise off-screen activities, Mix wound up performing trick riding and fancy shooting in the film. More movie work followed, and by 1913 Mix had worked his way up to starring in one- and two-reel Selig-Polyscope shorts, some of which he directed and wrote.

TOM MIX & SHOWMANSHIP

Grim-faced William Hart and his posse (top) go out with all guns blazing. Hart's last movie was *Tumbleweeds* in 1925. After that he ceded the golden Stetson to Tom Mix, and retired to his California estate, which is now open to the public; some visitors have reported spying Hart's ghost there. Tom Mix (opposite) punches out the baddie in *Rustler's Roundup* (1933). This was one of the series of talkies that Mix made for Universal, who lured him back to the screen from a lucrative second career with the Sells-Floto Circus.

After a hundred or so leading roles, some in five-reelers, Mix got his big break in 1917 when he signed with the more prestigious William Fox Studios. Playing the lead in five- to seven-reel features with bigger budgets, the charismatic Mix got to show off his wildest stunts against a backdrop of gorgeous Western scenery. In films like *A Western Masquerade*, Mix's vivid style brought the dime-novel cowboy to life, with a flashy wardrobe that took the pulps' colorful cover illustrations one step further. His witty on-screen personality added hefty doses of humor to his cliff-hangers, many of which were filmed in spectacular locations, such as the Grand Canyon. In 1926's *The Great K & A Train Robbery*, for example, Mix manages to escape from a cable stretched over Colorado's Grand Gorge, sliding down the high wire and landing on his loyal horse, Tony, which he claimed to have bought for $12.50. An excellent rider and athlete, Mix did most of his own stunts, specializing in fighting atop moving train cars. Mix only starred in one film that wasn't a Western, 1925's *Dick Turpin*, in which he played a swashbuckler; the movie flopped.

The greater a star he became, the more Mix formalized his cowboy character, ensuring his role-model status for the kids in his audience. He didn't drink, smoke, or cuss, and though his character depended on his fists, he rarely fired his gun to kill. By the mid-1920s, Mix earned $17,000 a week and was America's most famous movie star.

Other studios were constantly trying to come up with the next Tom Mix or Bill Hart. In 1923, to compete with Mix, FBO (Film Booking Office, the studio that later became RKO) hired Fred Thomson, who became known for his agility and good looks. The California-born Thomson, an accomplished athlete, had attended a seminary to become a

preacher, but he gave up the ministry and served in World War I. His press agents claimed that his switch to movies was due to his desire to set a good example to America's youth. His handsome face, wholesome demeanor, and he-man attributes earned him fans galore through such films as 1926's six-reeler *The Two Gun Man*, in which he uses his wits to retrieve his stolen cattle from rustlers and rescue his kidnapped girlfriend. He also played the lead in "historical" features about such figures as Kit Carson and Jesse James; his clean-cut portrayal of James left out the bank robberies. Thomson got himself a trusty stallion named Silver King from the Los Angeles Fire Department. Starring in *Thundering Hoofs*, the gifted Silver King managed to bury a body, then place a wreath and cross on the grave site before returning to his master. Sadly, Thomson himself met an early death when he was stricken with pneumonia in 1928.

Young Tom Mix (above) crouches tight-lipped over his faithful four-legged friend, Old Blue, in a two-reeler from 1918. Between 1909 and 1929, Mix made 326 silent movies of varying lengths, first for Selig Polyscope, then for Fox Studios, where he became a superstar, and finally for FBO. He is credited as director and scriptwriter on some of them. Fred Thomson (above) made an improbably clean-cut Jesse James in Paramount-Lasky's scrubbed-up biopic of 1927. College football player and one-time pastor, Thomson died tragically young (38) but his horse, Silver King, went on to forge an independent career as an equine movie star.

SERIES VERSUS EPIC WESTERNS

By the early 1920s, Westerns were evolving stylistically into two completely separate camps. "Series Westerns," also known as "program Westerns" or "programmers," were frequently made on a shoestring by independents, and starred the same actor playing the same character in movie after movie. Inspired by the models established by Broncho Billy, Bill Hart, and Tom Mix movies, the pictures all had similar plots and structures. They typically opened with a fistfight or gunplay, followed by a big horseback chase scene. The hero then unraveled whatever crime had taken place—stolen cattle, murdered rancher, kidnapped damsel—before the movie came to a climax with a dramatic shoot-out or showdown. For the starring role, the movie studios used tried-and-true favorites or occasionally introduced a new face to kick off yet another series of Westerns.

In the 1920s, these series Westerns ran four to six reels and lasted about 60 minutes or so. In the trades, these films gave birth to the terms "oaters,"

64

On location in Snake Valley, Nevada, James Cruze captures figures in a landscape in his landmark ten-reeler, *The Covered Wagon*, the genre's first silent epic, made for Famous Players-Lasky Studios. Cruze, who took up directing after a broken leg put an end to his acting aspirations, became the industry's highest-paid director and did not confine himself to Western themes.

"horse operas," and "shoot-'em-ups." In the 1930s, they evolved into B-Westerns, the name given to the shorter, budget pictures that played on double bills with more expensive A-movies. B-movies, often made by independents known as Poverty Row studios, were usually shown at America's small-town and rural theaters.

The other type of Western was the epic. These movies evolved from the early spectaculars made by Thomas Ince and directed by Biograph's D. W. Griffith (the latter by the mid-teens having abandoned Westerns for "message" pictures like *Intolerance*). Some later stars and directors actually cut their teeth by working on Griffith films as

extras and assistants, among them Harry Carey and directors John Ford and Cecil B. DeMille. Epics extended to many reels, with a running time as long as 120 minutes or more, and were filmed on location. Rather than use a big-name star, epics more often employed as many extras, horses, cattle, and wagons as necessary to tell the story, which usually centered around actual historic events in the West. In 1923, James Cruze directed the first lengthy (ten reels), lavish Western, *The Covered Wagon*. This film cost an exorbitant amount for the day—$782,000—and was filmed on location in the West. One famous scene, featuring hundreds of wagons and extras on horseback, depicted the Land Rush of 1849. Audiences were bedazzled by its

FORD-11-127

panoramic photography, which made the movie a huge success, and influenced an increase in longer-reel, large-scale Westerns. Cruze's next Western, *The Pony Express* (1925), didn't fare as well.

The most notable picture to follow *The Covered Wagon* was John Ford's first great epic Western of 1924, *The Iron Horse*. Born to Irish immigrant parents in Portland, Maine, Ford had begun his career in 1917 with two-reel Westerns starring Harry Carey. Establishing himself as the preeminent Western director, he made twenty films over a two-year period, some of which starred Tom Mix. Though not yet the master of his art, his visual sense, storytelling techniques, and success at putting actors through their paces were turning him into an extraordinary director. Two hours and forty minutes long, *The Iron Horse* told the story of the building of the railroad and was the longest film Ford ever made, containing 1,280 scenes and 275 subtitles. Filmed entirely in the Nevada desert, the spectacular starred the then unknown actor George O'Brien, a stuntman who'd worked as Mix's assistant cameraman. To add to the film's authenticity, Ford included original props: the real nineteenth-century trains Jupiter and 116, Wild Bill Hickok's Derringer, Horace "Go West Young Man" Greeley's actual stagecoach, and Bullet (for O'Brien), the horse that had won the title "Champion Pony Express Horse" for winning a race between St. Louis and San Francisco. After 1926's *Three Bad Men*, Ford didn't make another Western for nearly thirteen years.

Though epics remained popular with audiences, the sheer expense of making these pictures limited their production, compared with the cheapo series Westerns, which proliferated. Both types of film, however, served to establish the genre as pure American cinema in the mid-1920s, while prolonging the life of the Wild West in the public's imagination.

John Ford's first epic, *The Iron Horse*, made for Fox Studios, established his signature vocabulary of big themes, wide vistas, and impressive casting. A fictional love story is woven into the historical fact of the building of the transcontinental railroad, half a century before James Cameron picked up the trick for *Titanic*.

67

McCoy, Gibson, Jones, & Maynard

When making *The Covered Wagon*, James Cruze hired an Indian sign language expert and technical advisor named Colonel Tim McCoy as a liaison for the five hundred Native American extras on the film. McCoy originally hailed from Saginaw, Michigan; in 1912, after studying history at college, he left home to travel west. The expert horseman and astute student of Western and Native American lore settled on a Wyoming homestead, where he became acquainted with the Shoshone and Arapahoe tribes. After a stint in World War I, he began working for the Wyoming Indian Bureau, which led to his work on *The Covered Wagon*. McCoy, like Hart before him, decided that Westerns needed a strong dose of authenticity—and who better to provide it than himself? His flinty-eyed stare became his trademark when he began acting in movies, initially MGM's *The Thundering Herd*, before taking up starring roles. He strove for realism in his portrayals, costumes, and sets, but was often at the mercy of the economy-minded studios. One company, for example, shot two McCoy features concurrently. It was not unusual at the time to immediately follow up a Western with another one filmed with the actor on the same sets and location, but in this situation McCoy had to shuttle from one set to the other, to film two different movies at the same time. (The doubled-up films were produced by then fledgling filmmaker David O. Selznick, whose cost-cutting measures were intended to impress his studio bosses.)

Offering audiences yet another distinctive persona was Ed "Hoot" Gibson, a Nebraskan who reportedly got his nickname from his childhood hobby of hunting owls. A superb rider who was named All-Around Champion Cowboy at the 1912 Pendleton Roundup, Gibson spent several years as a movie wrangler and stuntman at Bison 101. For playing a cavalryman shot off his horse, he was

The Real McCoy (Tim McCoy), the stickler for authenticity who really did ride the prairies and study Native American languages and culture before launching his movie career with *The Thundering Herd* (1925). His career spanned 40 years and he appeared in more than 90 movies.

paid $5; for riding bareback as an "Indian" he got only $2.50, because falling off when riding bareback was easier than spilling out of a saddle. He doubled for Harry Carey a number of times, before serving in World War I. Finally, in 1919, he was given his own series at Universal, where he worked with John Ford in 1921. He mastered the slightly goofy saddle-pal character, emphasized by a huge hat, toothy grin, and a kind of aw-shucks demeanor. In addition to his humorous portrayals in films like the comic Western *Chip of*

the Flying U (based on a popular Western novel), he occasionally played dramatic roles, such as Pony Express rider Bob Langdon in the epic *The Flaming Frontier*, a fictionalized account of Custer's Last Stand. Normally, though, Gibson's character rarely carried a gun. In one picture, *Hard Hombre*, his character was called Peaceful Patton, " 'cause his mother raised him not to fight." When Peaceful Patton is mistaken for a shoot-'em-up desperado, "Hard Hombre," all kinds of comical mayhem ensues.

Strong silent stuntrider Buck Jones made over 150 movies during his career. He was also producer on 23 of them, and directed three others. He licensed his name to a line of merchandise, including hats, shirts, and children's cowboy outfits, and in the 1930s he founded a national scout-type organization for boys called the Buck Jones Rangers.

Another enormously popular cowboy star was muscular Buck Jones, who also started as a stuntman, beginning at Fox in the 1920s. Born Charles Fredrick Gebhart in Vincennes, Indiana, in 1891, Jones debuted in show biz with the Miller Bros. 101 Ranch and Wild West Show, followed by a stint at the Ringling Brothers Circus. Jones became an extra at Fox, leading to his getting signed to the studio in 1920. When Mix began demanding pay increases, the studio tried to use Jones's imminent stardom as leverage against Mix—threatening to replace him with the newcomer. However, Jones's rugged looks and low-key acting style more closely resembled those of the fading William S. Hart than those of Mix, and his comic touch was borrowed from Hoot Gibson. In one later film, *White Eagle*, Jones played an Indian Pony Express rider with dignity and grace. The film included many close-ups of Jones racing along on his steed, filmed with a camera mounted on a vehicle traveling next to the horse—a technique called "running inserts."

Texan Ken Maynard was perhaps the most outrageous trick rider of the bunch. After leaving home at fourteen, Maynard became a featured rider with the Ringling Brothers Circus. He began starring in cheap independent series Westerns in 1923 before moving to more lavish features. The lantern-jawed Maynard was not much of an actor, but such stunts as riding standing astride two racing horses won him lots of fans. The many running inserts showed audiences that it was Maynard himself on his palomino, Tarzan, and no stuntman pulling off such heroics. One of the last new stars of the silent era, Maynard was cast as the lead during a period of transition from silents to talkies. Thus, some of his films were made to be sold to theaters as either silents or talkies, which resulted in extremely stilted dialogue being recorded separately and dubbed in. Some of Maynard's riding scenes were so exciting,

71

Tumbleweeds (1925) was silent star William Hart's last movie, and he made sure that it carried his stamp. He starred in it (as rootless ranger Don Carver) codirected it (without credit), and his company produced it. It was rereleased in 1939, with an extra eight-minute introduction that was filmed by Hart himself.

however, that the footage was later reused and edited into bigger-budget, sound features.

Indeed, the introduction of sound to movies in 1927 would greatly affect Westerns. Audiences clamored for new movies with spoken dialogue so they could experience the latest in technical innovation. Of course, Westerns of the Tom Mix variety focused more on action than on dialogue. What is more, moviemakers found it difficult to mike outdoor scenes so that dialogue was audible. Thus, few epic Westerns were created in the late 1920s, and the limited number of series Westerns were clumsily made while directors figured out how to deal with sound problems.

Cowboy stars also faced a new competitor for the public's imagination: aviation heroes, thanks to Charles Lindbergh's transatlantic flight. As a 1929 issue of *Photoplay* magazine declared, "Lindbergh has put the cowboy into the discard heap... the Western novel and motion picture heroes have slunk away into the brush, never to return. The cow ponies are retired to the pasture.... Tom Mix, Hoot Gibson, and Ken Maynard must swap horses for airplanes or go to the old actors' home."

But just as their characters would not give up without a fight, most cowboy actors did attempt to make the transition to talkies, some with more success than others. One who didn't try was William Hart. In his late fifties, he had already retired to his California ranch in 1925 after making *Tumbleweeds* that year. His character in that movie, pointing to a bevy of Oklahoma Land Rush settlers, utters the prophetic lines, "Boys, it's the last of the West."

The first official sound Western, *In Old Arizona*, appeared in 1929. It was directed by Raoul Walsh and featured the Cisco Kid, played by Warner Baxter. Tom Mix starred in a few more features up until 1933, but his voice lacked the appeal of his stunts, and he faded out after slumming it in a low-budget serial in 1935. Following a few years of touring with his own Wild West show and circus, he died in an Arizona car crash in 1940. Buck Jones made the transition into "talkies" with more ease than did Mix and went on to sustain a three-decade-long career, acting primarily in low-budget B's, as did Maynard, McCoy, and Gibson. (Maynard and Jones also operated their own Wild West shows when not filming.) Tragically, Jones burned to death in a 1942 fire at a Boston nightclub where he had been attempting to rescue those inside. Maynard and Gibson were kept afloat by independent B-movies but never regained the star status they'd enjoyed in the 1920s.

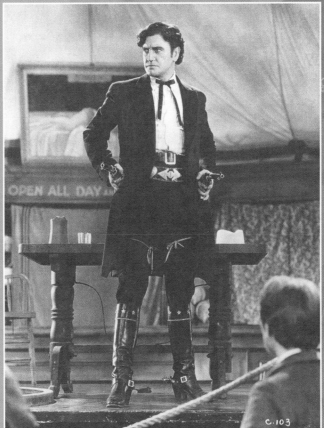

During the early 1930s, a few new Western features emerged from the major studios. King Vidor directed a William Hart–inspired *Billy the Kid* in 1930. It employed Hart as a technical advisor who lent a gun from his collection—one that had originally belonged to the Kid. The film ends happily, with Billy the Kid escaping across the Mexican border with his sweetheart. Raoul Walsh returned in 1930 with *The Big Trail*, starring for the first time a struggling B-actor named John Wayne. Wayne had already cut his teeth as a bit player in several John Ford silents, fashioning his rugged looks and plainly dressed image after his idol Harry Carey. At the end of the decade, Wayne would discover superstardom in the great Ford Western, *Stagecoach*.

Another epic was released in 1930, *Cimarron*, based on the Edna Ferber novel about the Oklahoma Land Rush; it became the first Western to win an Oscar. A 1932 production, *Law and Order*, cast Harry Carey as Doc Holliday and Walter Huston as Wyatt Earp. The public's fascination with outlaws and the Old West appeared to have ebbed, however, and neither film fared particularly well at the box office, despite that Oscar for *Cimarron*. The time had come for a new gimmick to woo audiences back to Westerns.

73

Johnny Mack Brown (opposite) made his first appearance as a Westerner in King Vidor's *Billy the Kid* (1930), in which a parallel-universe Billy gets away with his life and his girl. Richard Dix (above) is Yancey Cravat—lawyer, sheriff, newspaper proprietor, and snappy dresser in *Cimarron* (1930). Directed by Wesley Ruggles, it won the first Oscar for the Western genre but opinion is divided on its merits. Dix, RKO's in-house leading man, received a nomination for best actor.

74

Roy Rogers (above), the singing cowboy's Singing Cowboy, who persuaded the world that life in the West was one long wholesome singalong—after all, you can't pluck and shoot at the same time. All singin', all twirlin' stuntman and cowboy star Ken Maynard shows what he can do (opposite), supported by his rocklike horse, Tarzan.

Guns and Guitars
Gene Autry, Roy Rogers, and the Western Musical

IN THE EARLY 1930S, THE DEPRESSION DAMPENED THE PUBLIC'S ENTHUSIASM FOR WESTERNS. BUT SOON A NEW KIND OF STAR—THE SINGING COWBOY—BROUGHT AUDIENCES BACK IN DROVES, WHILE SPREADING THE POPULARITY OF WESTERN MUSIC ONTO THE RADIO AIRWAVES.

Westerns had been overtaken by gangster movies in audiences' imagination, with shoot-outs in smoky speakeasies replacing action on the open range.

Perhaps trying to rekindle excitement in his work, Ken Maynard decided to try something a little different in his 1930 Universal picture, *Sons of the Saddle*. An amateur musician and true lover of Western songs, Maynard warbled two tunes, "Trail Herd Song" and "Down the Home Trail with You." The musical interludes didn't attract much attention, however, except from Maynard's studio boss, who found his vocalizing too raspy. Undaunted, the would-be singing cowboy became the Fiddlin' Buckaroo in the 1933 film of the same name. In that year Maynard sang the title song for his picture *The Strawberry Roan*, still to no acclaim. Eventually, the M. M. Cole Publishing Company issued the cowboy hero's own songbook of favorite Western numbers, *Ken Maynard's Songs of the Trails*, which included the self-penned movie

title song "Wheels of Destiny," the theme song for *The Trail Herd*, and "Singin' on the Range." Shortly after, Columbia Records released four of his recordings.

Maynard's music may have inspired Lone Pine Productions' Paul Malvern, who in 1933 gave another B-player his chance to sing on-screen. John Wayne was tapped to play Singin' Sandy Saunders in a series of sixteen-program Westerns, beginning with *Riders of Destiny*. An undercover G-man-meets-cowboy character who had a way with a tune, Singin' Sandy did not strike a chord with gangster or Western movie audiences. To this day, there is disagreement as to whose voice was coming out of Wayne's mouth. One thing that is known for sure is that Wayne definitely did not play the guitar he feigned strumming. And years later his wife, Pilar, told reporters that the role made her embarrassed husband feel like a "pansy."

76

All questions of masculinity aside, something was in the air that was leading to a huge breakthrough in the B-Western movie. After such inauspicious beginnings, the musical Western blossomed in the mid-1930s, thanks largely to radio and recording star Gene Autry. At Republic Pictures, he single-handedly created a new subgenre of Western that remained a top box-office draw for nearly two decades. Gene Autry was the first of more than a dozen singing cowboy film stars, though only Autry and his Republic Pictures protégé Roy Rogers won huge success, with contenders—like Dick Foran and the talented Western baritone Tex Ritter—also garnering their share of fans. Others, usually established Western singers, played bit parts in straight B-Westerns, providing what became the mandatory musical interlude in oaters of the late 1930s and 1940s.

The Old Dodge City Cowboy Band (background), caught on camera *c.*1911. Members played in full cowboy gear, and the conductor used a six-shooter as a baton. Ken Maynard (above) is the eponymous Fiddlin' Buckaroo (1933). Dick Foran (opposite), Warner Bros' own babblin' buckaroo, serenades the sagebrush with a song entitled "Moonlight on the Prairie."

THE RISE OF GENE AUTRY

Like their predecessors in earlier program Westerns, singing cowboy film stars came from all over the map. Only a handful were actually born in the West or had backgrounds in cattlepunching and horse riding. Preeminent singing cowboy Gene Autry could legitimately be called a Westerner, however. Autry was born near Tioga, Texas, in 1907, to a struggling livestock dealer and his musical wife. Growing up in Texas and Oklahoma, Autry learned about horses (though he was definitely not keen on becoming a working cowhand) and how to play guitar. His grandfather enlisted him to sing in his Baptist church choir when Autry was only five. When he was twelve, he ordered his first guitar from the Sears catalog with money he'd saved baling hay for his uncle. He started playing and singing for tips at a local movie theater and barber shop; three years later he escaped the drudgery of farm work by running off with the Fields Brothers Marvelous Medicine Show. His family relocated to Oklahoma, and in the town of Chelsea he got a job as a telegraph operator for the Frisco Railroad. One fateful night, while Autry was singing and playing guitar on the job, the legendary Western humorist Will Rogers, a native of nearby Claremore, Oklahoma, stopped in to send a telegram. He liked what he heard and urged the young man to travel to New York to give show biz a whirl.

It took about a year after his conversation with Rogers for Autry to try his luck in New York. With a free pass from the railroad and his meager savings, he traveled to Manhattan in the winter of 1928 to make his fortune as an entertainer. An audition with a Victor recording executive resulted in the greenhorn entertainer being encouraged to return to Oklahoma, polish his chops, and come back when he had gained more experience as a professional singer. The man even gave Autry a letter of recommendation, which he used to land a spot on Tulsa radio station KVOO.

It was there that Autry began making a name for himself as Oklahoma's Yodelin' Cowboy. Gaining confidence and a following for his music, Autry hightailed it back to New York in 1929 and began recording for a number of labels. His repertoire included bluesy "hillbilly" numbers and Western songs like those collected by John Lomax in 1910. It was a sentimental cowrite with an old railroad buddy Jimmy Long, however, that garnered Autry his first smash, for the ARC label (which would become Columbia Records). "That Silver-Haired Daddy of Mine" was a plaintive pop ballad that had nothing to do with the Wild West—though it would be crooned by Autry in his first starring role. It sold a million copies, leading to Autry's star rising in the early 1930s as he became a featured performer on the influential *National Barn Dance* program on Chicago's megawatt radio station WLS. He also got his own *Conqueror Record Hour* show and began selling Gene Autry songbooks and guitars via station owner Sears Roebuck. As his Western music hits began to proliferate, Autry emphasized his cowboy

A publicity poster for Gene Autry's first musical Western, released by Republic Pictures in 1936, is shown above. Improbably neat and tidy and always impeccably dressed (opposite), Gene Autry (in white hat) and at his right his comical sidekick Frog Millhouse (Smiley Burnette) look serious in Joseph Kane's *The Old Barn Dance* (1938), a comedy musical with guns. The cast included a youthful Roy Rogers, under his previous name of Dick Weston.

image, wearing more ornate embroidered shirts, decorative boots, and a wide-brimmed Stetson hat. Other stars on the show, such as Patsy Montana, Louise Massey and the Westerners, and the Girls of the Golden West, also helped to popularize the image of cowpokes, along with their music.

Movies ෨ Go ෨ Musical

In 1934 Autry headed to Hollywood for the first time. It's unclear just whose idea it was to give Autry a chance in the movies. Some film historians have reported that Autry sent letters about himself to Republic Pictures president Herbert Yates, proposing that he get a shot in Tinseltown. Art Satherley, head of Autry's label (which had business connections with Republic), had close ties to Yates and Republic producer Nat Levine and later took credit for bringing Autry to their attention. In any case, whoever came up with the idea was a genius. Once again, Ken Maynard was instrumental in the development of the musical Western: his starring feature, *In Old Santa Fe*, first presented Gene Autry on-screen as a performer singing at a barn dance. Audiences loved it. The idea was hatched to make an entire Western with Autry playing himself and singing cowboy songs throughout. He first had to pay his dues, however, starring in a wacky sci-fi-meets-Western serial called *The Phantom Empire*, where the cowboy hero battled Martians living in a cavern city underneath a dude ranch where Autry resided.

In 1935 Autry made his first full-fledged musical Western, *Tumbling Tumbleweeds*. The title came from a recent Autry hit song, which was included in the movie, along with "Silver-Haired Daddy" and six other songs. The movie bowled over audiences and studio execs—and a new cinematic sensation was underway. Early on, Autry's Westerns developed a successful format and stuck to it. Along with the music, they featured a large dose of action and

comedy, the latter provided by Autry's sidekick Smiley "Frog" Burnette, a multi-instrumentalist (who excelled at one-man-bandmanship) and songwriter. With his clean-living, fancy-dressing cowboy, Autry expanded on the character played by Tom Mix. He developed a cowboy code that urged youngsters to be kind to animals and old people and to treat people of all races and creeds fairly.

Except for a couple of early movies, like the cavalry-versus-Indians picture *Ride, Ranger, Ride*, Autry's films took place in the "modern-day" West, where Gene and company rode horses while their adversaries took advantage of technology's tools such as planes, cars, and radio. "To offset expected criticisms that this new brand of musical Western was a travesty of tradition," explains film historian William K. Everson, "Republic set them in their own never-never land, placing them quite apart from other Westerns." Like most B-Westerns, the plot lines were usually interchangeable, but Autry films did offer a more progressive role for women, playing characters who were strong-willed and freethinking rather than damsels in distress. The plots sometimes involved contemporary social problems such as environmental pollution and injustices suffered by small farmers, Native Americans, and Latinos. Autry—often playing an entertainer, as in *The Old Barn Dance*—would break into song at the beginning and end of the picture. Sometimes the music frequently helped to resolve the crisis in some way—even more so than gunplay and violence, which were downplayed.

Indeed, the films featured one hit song after another, acting as a sort of precursor to music videos. Rural kids flocked to the Saturday afternoon matinees to see good triumph over evil in *Melody Trail*, *The Big Show*, *The Old Corral*, *Rootin' Tootin' Rhythm*, *Yodelin' Kid from Pine Ridge*, *Public Cowboy #1*, and *Man from*

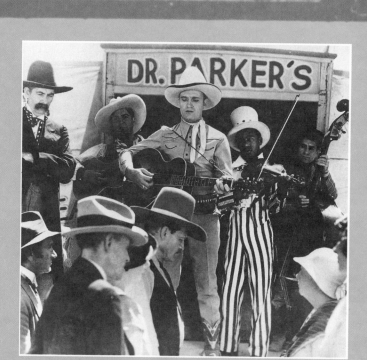

To offset expected criticisms that this new brand of musical Western was a travesty of tradition, Republic set them in their own never-never land, placing them quite apart from other Westerns.

Rovin' Tumbleweeds (directed by George Sherman, 1939) showcased Autry as a singing cowboy congressman (opposite) confronting corrupt politicians standing in the way of flood control legislation; Chinatown with a twang. Autry and his band (right) play in his first movie, *Tumbling Tumbleweeds* (1935), named for one of his early songs.

Music Mountain. Meanwhile, their parents bought Autry's recordings to fantasize about the freedom of the West's wide-open spaces in songs such as "Mexicali Rose," "South of the Border," "Back in the Saddle Again," and "When It's Springtime in the Rockies." Autry backed up the fantasies by constantly making personal appearances and trying to publicly live up to his cowboy code.

By 1940, Gene Autry was one of the most popular—and busiest—entertainers in America, making six to eight movies and numerous new recordings annually, appearing all over the United States and Britain when not recording or filming, and starring in his own CBS network radio show, *Melody Ranch*.

After enlisting and serving for four years in World War II, Autry took over the reins of his acting career. He ended his relationship with Republic and formed his own Flying A Productions, distributed by Columbia. These slightly more realistic films found Autry dressed down in blue jeans rather than in resplendent shirts worn with pants tucked into fancy boots. In 1950, when Autry saw that the future was a little black box in America's living rooms, Autry's Flying A Productions began making Gene Autry television shows, which featured more action and less music. His touring, moviemaking, and recording continued unabated. Around this time, he also stumbled onto a new format: seasonal songs. Autry cowrote "Here Comes Santa Claus," then recorded "Rudolph the Red-Nosed Reindeer," giving Christmas songs a Western twang.

Gene Autry and the boys serenade the dogies (and each other), creating the unshakeable myth of the campfire singalong (below). Autry, who had started performing as a teenager, was so popular that his movies inspired good-natured parody. City slicker Dick Powell (opposite), better known as a Busby Berkeley crooner and urban matinee idol, serenades his sweetheart in *Cowboy from Brooklyn* (1938, directed by Lloyd Bacon).

OTHER CROONING COWPOKES

Two months after Autry's first feature in 1935, Warner Bros. offered up its version of a singing cowboy in the person of New Jersey–born Dick Foran, in *Moonlight on the Prairie*. The studio must have been on the same wavelength as Republic but was beaten to the punch. And Autry's authenticity as a rural Westerner gave him a huge edge over the operatic-voiced, Princeton-educated Foran. It was hard enough to buy a cowboy riding his horse while playing guitar and singing, but doing so with a trained, vaudeville-style voice just didn't cut it. Though Foran would star in a dozen features—including 1937's *Cowboy from Brooklyn*—many with his palomino horse Smoke, he never approached Autry's success.

Throughout Autry's reign as Public Cowboy #1, the various studios tried to compete with their own singing buckaroos. In the late 1930s, a number of short-lived singing cowboys were showcased. A few, such as Fred Scott (billed as the "Silvery Voiced Baritone") and Bob Baker (born Leland "Tumble" Weed), actually came from the West and knew their way around horses—and a Western song. Baker passed a screen test after his mother sent a Hollywood studio her son's photograph and credentials as a bona fide buckaroo. Others, such as New Jersey–born George Houston and Pennsylvanian James Newill, were opera-singing actors coaxed into going Western. Some, including Jimmy Wakely, Ray Whitely, and Art Davis, began their careers strictly as Western musicians, crossed paths with Autry and got work in his pictures, and eventually starred in a few of their own.

Texas native Tex Ritter was in a class all his own. In the mid-1920s, while attending law school at the University of Texas at Austin, he became fascinated by Western folk songs and learned a number of authentic cowboy ballads. After college he moved to New York, where in 1930 he acted on Broadway in *Green Grow the Lilacs*, the predecessor to the smash Broadway musical *Oklahoma*. He next sang with the Lone Star Rangers on a New York radio show, followed by a stint on a children's radio program, *Cowboy Tom's Roundup*, then, finally, his own *Tex Ritter's Campfire* show. By the early 1930s he had gotten a record deal on ARC (Autry's label) and scored a hit, "Rye Whiskey," with his distinctive twangy baritone. Hollywood came calling in 1936, and Ritter acted in the musical Western *Song of the Gringo*, the first of twenty low-budget oaters. Ritter and his horse White Flash moved from studio to studio, including Monogram, Grand National, Columbia, Universal, and PRC. Meanwhile, he continued to record hits, making Western songs nationally popular, including "Jingle, Jangle, Jingle" (on Capitol Records) and "Blood on the Saddle." His title song for the classic *High Noon* won an Oscar in 1952.

Hittin' the Trail (1937) is an early Ritter vehicle in which he is mistaken for a gunslinger, The Tombstone Kid, but for Woodard Maurice (aka Tex) Ritter, the music came first. A collector at academic level of authentic traditional Western songs, he established a successful radio career in 1930. His first movie wasn't made until 1936. Once in the saddle, Ritter went on to make 85 movies, 78 of them Westerns. A poster for *King of the Cowboys*, directed in 1943 by Joseph Kane, is shown opposite. Rogers was now an established star, and became known as the king of the cowboys on and off screen. *Under Western Stars* (1938), the movie that made a star of Roy Rogers, is shown in the background, opposite. The cast included Rogers's horse Trigger and Smiley Burnette.

ROY ROGERS, KING OF THE COWBOYS

Meanwhile, during Autry's military service from 1942 to 1946, Republic Pictures pushed another of its singing cowboys into the spotlight, eventually naming him King of the Cowboys (the label originally created for Tom Mix). Roy Rogers was born Leonard Slye in Cincinnati, Ohio, in 1911, and raised the son of a shoe-factory worker in nearby Duck Run, Ohio. He first tried show biz after his family joined other Depression-era poor folks in the migration to California. There, the superb yodeler formed a succession of singing groups, first with his cousin as the Slye Brothers, then with the formidable and prolific Western songwriter Bob Nolan. Nolan's many compositions include two of the best and most famous cowboy songs of all time, "Tumbling Tumbleweeds" and "Cool Water." After a number of shifting lineups and name changes—including the Rocky Mountaineers, the O-Bar-O Cowboys, and the

Pioneers—Nolan (baritone), Slye (lead), and Tim Spencer (tenor) formed the harmony-singing and yodeling Pioneer Trio in 1934. Rechristened by a radio announcer as the Sons of the Pioneers, the group soon garnered background work adding musical interludes to B-Westerns, including some Gene Autry pictures. Slye even got a few lines in 1936's *The Old Corral*, as well as an exciting tumble-down-the-hill fight scene with Autry. At different times the Sons of the Pioneers included among its members the superb instrumentalists and longtime Rogers backup musicians Hugh Farr on fiddle and Karl Farr on lead guitar; vocalist Pat Brady, who would later play Rogers's sidekick in some films and television shows; and Ken Curtis, who'd briefly been a singing cowboy himself (and best known later as Festus on *Gunsmoke*). After Slye moved on to become a star, the Sons of the Pioneers

85

"Happy Trails"
Roy Rogers & Trigger

continued to make successful recordings, movies, and appearances for decades.

Renamed Roy Rogers—having shed the stage name Dick Weston—the singer replaced Gene Autry in the 1938 picture *Under Western Stars*. Autry had walked out on Republic, demanding more pay and better film distribution practices from the studio. After Autry mended fences with Republic, Rogers became second banana at the studio, which meant getting smaller-budget films—often simply remaking earlier Autry pictures—and less impressive songs. He was catching on with audiences, however, as illustrated by one 1941 fan magazine article, "From Hillbilly to Hero." Here, the slightly built and, as he described himself, "squinty-eyed" Rogers was described glowingly: "Except that his all-cowboy wardrobe is a little snappier than most, he's the type of unspoiled, unaffected, happy-go-lucky young Westerner you might meet on any colorful ranch."

Just as Autry had his gorgeous chestnut Champion, Rogers's pal was the talented palomino Trigger, who became the focus of some pictures. In *Trigger Jr.*, for example, Rogers takes the rap for killing a rival rancher's horse

and goes to jail to save Trigger, who'd been accused of the killing. Trigger is eventually exonerated and returns from hiding after a mare gives birth to his colt, Trigger Jr.

Some early Rogers oaters found the likable actor being cast as such historical characters as Billy the Kid, Jesse James, and Buffalo Bill. In 1941's *Jesse James at Bay*, he actually played two roles, Jesse and another outlaw named Clint Burns.

After Autry enlisted in the Air Force in 1942, Republic dubbed Rogers "King of the Cowboys" (made official in the 1943 film *King of the Cowboys*). Some of his 1942–1943 films are among his best, including *Heart of the Golden West* and *Silver Spurs*. As the budgets were raised to allot more money to his films than had ever been spent on Autry's, so the splashy musical interludes and fancy costumes multiplied. Gradually,

the action ingredients were cut almost entirely, and the interaction between Rogers and his female costar Dale Evans was emphasized, in such Westerns as *The Cowboy and the Senorita*, the first to pair Rogers and Evans. Apparently, after Republic's president Herbert Yates saw *Oklahoma* on Broadway in the early 1940s, he insisted on the Rogers–Evans movies becoming more like the musical. Romance between Rogers and Evans sparked in real life, and they were married in 1947. After a private ceremony, they married again in a theater in Ardmore, Oklahoma, where the public could buy tickets and attend.

After the war, Rogers's film budgets steadily shrank, with action scenes gradually replacing musical numbers. Rogers remained popular and won even more young fans when he and Evans began starring in a weekly television show in November 1951 and continued appearing at rodeos and Western shows.

The glorious Trigger (opposite) was almost as famous as his rider, costarring in all Roy Rogers's movies. He died in 1965 at the grand old age of 33. Backed up with guns and rope, Rogers (above) plays a cattleman trying to ship his stock by riverboat in *Heart of the Golden West* (1942, directed by Joseph Kane). There was still plenty of time for a song.

The Last of the Singing Cowboys

Following World War II, singing cowboy pictures began to lose their luster. Kids started getting into sci-fi pictures, while returning GIs were more interested in realism than fantasy entertainment. Though audiences for musical Westerns were shrinking, the studios continued to search for new stars. After playing bit parts in Autry and Rogers pictures, Texas-born Eddie Dean, a former *National Barn Dance* performer, began starring in such movies as 1945's *Song of Old Wyoming*, the first musical Western to be filmed in a new Cinecolor system that did not catch on. Dean's acting style itself, though, was fairly colorless.

Fellow Texan Monte Hale almost replaced Rogers in 1945 when Republic thought he was going into the service. Hale had been discovered while participating in a war bond drive in Texas. Summoned to Hollywood for a screen test, Hale eventually played the occasional lead in latter-day singing Westerns, but mostly took supporting roles. In 1956 he acted in George Stevens's epic drama *Giant*, which starred James Dean, Rock Hudson, Elizabeth Taylor, and Hale's buddy Chill Wills.

The last of the breed was Rex Allen, who did get to replace Rogers as Republic's final singing cowboy. Like Rogers and Autry, he often played "himself,"

sometimes a rodeo star or entertainer. The Arizona-born Western singer had a down-home, pleasant voice somewhat similar to Autry's and Rogers's. His career began with the 1950 vehicle *The Arizona Cowboy*, in which he played a rodeo rider out to exonerate his father who'd been unfairly accused of a crime. As well as singing, Allen got to show off his trick riding and roping skills. He starred in eighteen more Western musicals, which for the most part had all the hallmarks of the format that Gene Autry had perfected nearly twenty years before. In such films as *Rodeo King and the Senorita* (featuring a young Buddy Ebsen), Allen rides his fabulous steed Koko—"the Miracle Horse of the Movies"—to defeat the villains, all while strumming a guitar, singing a song, and winning the admiration of his leading lady.

Through their music—much of which is available today on CD—the singing cowboys live on. Douglas B. "Ranger Doug" Green, leader of the Grammy award-winning singing-cowboy group Riders in the Sky, expresses it this way: "The indelible legacy of the singing cowboy is a naive innocence that America has always prized in itself, a stirring version of the American dream, and a great deal of the finest music to branch from that magnificent shade tree we call country music."

Rex Allen, shown with his cowboy family (above), inherited Roy Rogers's white hat and guitar, and was the last singing cowboy out of the stable. Eddie Dean (opposite) came in late on the musical Western wave, signing with Republic Pictures in 1938. His first starring role was in *Song of Old Wyoming*—in which he became the first B-Western movie star to appear in color—and he made 19 more movies, all of which also starred his horse, Flash.

Jim Brown (above) as lawman Lyedecker in *100 Rifles* (directed by Tom Gries, 1969) on the trail of Burt Reynolds's Indian freedom fighter. Blaxploitation comes to the prairies in *The Black Bounty Hunter* (1974), directed by Jack Arnold and originally released as *Boss Nigger*. It starred Fred Williamson (right) who also wrote and produced it.

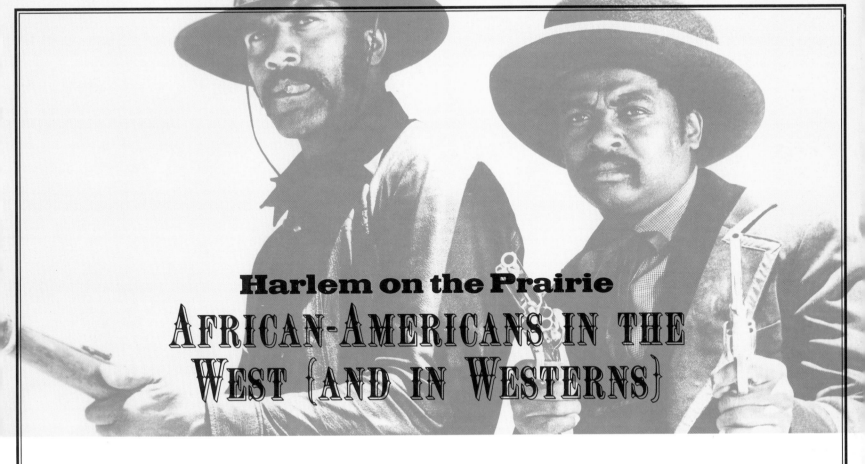

Harlem on the Prairie
AFRICAN-AMERICANS IN THE WEST (AND IN WESTERNS)

WITH ITS PROMISE OF FREEDOM AND OPPORTUNITY, THE WEST BECKONED THOUSANDS OF BRAVE AND RESTLESS SOULS LOOKING FOR A NEW BEGINNING AND A BETTER LIFE. AMONG THOSE HEEDING THE CALL WERE AFRICAN-AMERICANS SEEKING THE INDEPENDENCE AND ECONOMIC POSSIBILITIES THAT HAD BEEN DENIED THEM UNDER SLAVERY.

Some had their hopes dashed by unforeseen hardships and more racism; others overcame these barriers and reinvented their lives—some as cowboys.

According to an 1852 census, even before the Civil War, as many as two thousand blacks lived in California. Discrimination had prevented most from participating in the Gold Rush, but they found other means of employment. By 1860, 2,827 African-American men lived in California, primarily in cities. In Texas, after the end of the war between the states and at the beginning of the cattle drives, ranchers enlisted many black cowboys. About a quarter of the former slave state's white men had been killed or wounded in the war, leaving plenty of opportunity for freed African-Americans, many of whom had already

worked with livestock during slavery. An estimated five thousand black cowboys eventually rode herd on the Chisholm Trail.

On the open range, discrimination against blacks subsided. All men were created equal on a drive, as long as they could handle their share of the work, and many black cowboys excelled at it. On a typical trail drive, two members of an eight-man crew would be black, and as months passed friendships and understanding were forged. Once range riders reached the cow town, however, the status quo was maintained: black buckaroos congregated at one end of the bar in saloons and weren't allowed in some brothels. The first cowboy killed in Dodge City, in fact, was a black man named Tex who got caught in cross fire between two white desperadoes. The first victims of gunslingers John Wesley Hardin and Clay Allison were black, too.

Still, as the nineteenth century progressed, racism and bigotry did not stop the flow of African-American pioneers. Between 1870 and 1910, from twenty thousand to forty thousand black homesteaders, or "exodusters," migrated to Kansas. The black population in western territories doubled during this period, reaching nearly a million by 1910.

Nat Love, or Deadwood Dick (opposite), one of the few buckaroos to pen an autobiography, worked as cowboy, Indian fighter, rodeo rider, and, in his final years, pullman porter. John Ford's *Sergeant Rutledge* (1960), shown in the background, is the story of a black army officer accused of rape, told in flashback. Woody Strode played the eponymous sergeant.

BUFFALO SOLDIERS

Beginning in the late 1860s, some black men moved west with the military as part of two cavalry and two infantry regiments known as Buffalo Soldiers. Native Americans gave them the name because to their eyes an African-American man's hair looked like a buffalo mane. One cavalry unit took the buffalo as its symbol, proudly carrying a flag emblazoned with a bison. Though Buffalo Soldiers received inferior horses, supplies, equipment, and food, they had a much lower desertion rate than white troops. They were often sent to the most isolated outposts, but took part in all the major skirmishes of the "winning" of the West.

NAT LOVE

93

The most famous nineteenth-century African-American cowboy was the flamboyant Nat Love, an early Wild West show and rodeo star who liked to dress in chaps and a uniquely styled hat with a turned-up brim. Born and raised a slave in Tennessee, he moved west after the Civil War, finding work punching cattle on the northern plains. He became renowned for his roping and riding skills; his fame became such that he wrote *The Life and Adventures of Nat Love, Better Known in Cattle Country as "Deadwood Dick," by Himself*. In this dime novel–style autobiography Love described his many exploits, including taking credit for being the real Deadwood Dick (he first gained recognition for his showmanship at an 1876 roping contest in Deadwood, South Dakota). More than any of his exciting escapades, though, Love most relished the respect he gained from his fellow buckaroos, writing in his book that he valued "last but foremost the friends I have made and the friends I have gained."

AFRICAN-AMERICANS IN WESTERNS

In spite of their presence in the real West, African-American cowboys historically were not represented in Westerns. There were some black actors, but rather than portraying homesteaders or broncho busters, they played servants in films ranging from *Cimarron* in 1930 to *Jesse James* in 1939. These roles maintained stereotypes, prevalent in other types of films, that had been established by earlier forms of entertainment such as vaudeville and minstrel shows.

BILL PICKETT, KING OF THE BULL-DOGGERS

In the meantime, as movies increased in popularity during the 1920s, a niche opened for black films to entertain African-American audiences. Particularly in the segregated South, movie houses that opened in black neighborhoods needed material. In the 1920s, the Norman Film Manufacturing Company—a studio based in Jacksonville, Florida—began shooting Westerns featuring all-black casts to fill those theaters. The white-owned studio actively recruited African-American directors and actors from vaudeville and stage. One of the very first black rodeo idols, Bill Pickett, was enlisted to star in two Norman films—*The Crimson Skull* and *The Bull-dogger*: Pickett actually invented the rodeo sport of "bull-dogging," which later came to be known as steer wrestling.

During the course of his exciting life, Bill Pickett broke down many barriers. Of black and Native American descent, he was born in 1870 in Texas, where he became a cowhand after the fifth grade. In 1903, he saw a bulldog—a breed often used by ranchers to help herd cattle—leap upon a steer, bite down on its lip, and force it to submit. Pickett decided to try the technique himself. He would ride alongside a steer, drop to the beast's head, and twist its head slowly toward the sky. Pickett would then bite the steer's lip (some sources say upper lip, others say lower), which enabled him to render the longhorn helpless. This incredible feat and his skill on horseback led to Pickett's being featured in the pulp *Leslie's Illustrated Weekly* in 1905 and joining the Miller Bros. 101 Ranch Wild West troupe two years later. There, astride his horse Spradley, Pickett performed his risky strategy for subduing fierce longhorn steers, in the process popularizing a new category in rodeos and Wild West shows. Eventually, as bull-dogging became more widespread, rodeo cowpunchers performed the feat without biting the steer's lip. Pickett gained even more celebrity in 1908 by wrestling a charging bull in Mexico City.

Even so, in the early days of his career in American rodeos, Pickett had to pass himself off as Hispanic, wearing a vaquero's rig because African-Americans had been banned from participating in most rodeos. Eventually, Pickett's popularity eliminated such discriminatory practices and today there are several African-American rodeo associations, including the Bill Pickett Invitational Rodeo.

94

The Norman Film Manufacturing Company enlisted Pickett to star in the film named after the rodeo act he created. The company promoted *The Bull-dogger* (1923) with lobby cards and ads that billed Pickett as "the Colored Hero" who performed "Death Defying Feats of Courage and Skill." The poster showed the handsome Pickett looking gallant in flowing neckerchief, leather wrist gauntlets, and large-brimmed Stetson. The film's press book described *The Bull-dogger* as including "fancy and trick riding by black cowboys and cowgirls and bull-dogging and throwing with their teeth the wildest of the wild steers on the Mexican border. This is the first feature picture of its kind and proves conclusively that the black cowboy is capable of doing anything the white cowboy does." There wasn't much of a plot, but the audiences loved it.

In 1923 Pickett was also featured in Norman's first all-black Western thriller, *The Crimson Skull*. With a little more of a typical shoot-'em-up plot, the "baffling Western mystery photoplay," according to its promotional material, starred the stage actors Anita Bush and Lawrence Chenault (the latter taking three roles). It also featured "the one-legged marvel Steve Reynolds and 30 colored cowboys, produced in the all-colored city of Boley, Okla." The five-reeler's plot revolves around a vicious desperado known as the Skull (because he dons a hooded skeleton suit), and his band of Terrors who take over a town by intimidating the sheriff. The hero, Bob Calem (one of Chenault's roles), tries to trick the bandits by pretending to be an outlaw himself and infiltrating their ranks. The climax occurs when Calem is accused by some of the gang of being a traitor. To test his loyalty the outlaws apply the "test of the Crimson Skull," in which, according to the press book, "one drop of blood decides his fate, if he shall live or die."

95

Bill Pickett (1870–1932), son of a former slave, joined the Miller Bros. 101 Ranch show (far left in background picture) in 1905. His self-taught art of bull-dogging (steer wrestling) was brought to the silver screen in a film that was more documentary than fiction (above), opening the door for further Westerns with more traditional storylines.

ON LOCATION IN BOLEY, ★ OKLAHOMA ★

The Norman Company set up production in Boley, which was the largest all-black town in America at the time. One black newspaper of the day described Boley as "a thriving municipality, owning its own electric light plant and modern water works…contain[ing] two modern and up-to-date cotton gins and one of our few national banks." A 1923 article in the African-American paper the *Cleveland Gazette* praised the producers for sparing no expense to "make it a typical picture of the old swash-buckling west, with the added attraction of a cast composed of our actors and actresses who could ride and shoot in true Western style…. Real Afro-American cowboys were secured in Boley. These were ranchers who owned their own mounts and could ride like the wind. Their dare-devil riding and handling of the six-gun prove them excelled by none…. In one scene, over a thousand head of cattle are shown being rounded up by our own cowboys…." The *Gazette* critic also commended the performances: "Steve Reynolds, the one-legged marshal, is in this picture and proves that he can do thrilling stunts that a two-legged man can't do. With nothing but his trusty wooden leg to defend him and the sheriff's daughter against the Skull and his gang of Hooded Terrors, he found their way to freedom and did a piece of wild riding that proves he is a marvel. His usual funny stunts prove him a natural-born comedian. Bill Pickett, our veteran world's champion bull dogger, proves that he is one of the greatest trained riders and ropers that the West has produced and does stunts that call for real skill. As the sheriff's deputy, he helps solve a baffling mystery." *Billboard* writer J. A. Jackson pointed out

in 1923 that "many of our race, and even many of the general public, are unaware that some of the most proficient riders and ropers of the range are colored men. Some few of these have appeared from time to time with the different circuses, but the public has regarded them as exceptions, whereas riders are common in the vicinity of Boley."

Norman and a few other companies that made black films ran into financial trouble when the Depression hit in 1929. In the meantime, Pickett and fellow buckaroo Nat Love had opened the doors for cowboys of color. Pickett traveled the world, winning acclaim as a performer, but his dangerous profession finally got the best of him. In 1932, at the age of seventy-three, he died from injuries sustained while breaking broncs at the 101 Ranch in Oklahoma.

THE BRONZE BUCKAROO

By the late 1930s the Western's revival via the singing cowboy was in full swing. Gene Autry and those who followed in his footsteps had gained many admirers, including an African-American vocalist with the Earl Hines Band in Chicago. Musically talented Herbert Jeffries, born in 1912 in Detroit, decided to try his luck in Hollywood in 1937. Having recorded a few sides with Hines, he got a gig as a singer and emcee at L.A.'s Club Alabam. He was contacted by Jed Buell of Associated Features, who wanted to create an all-black musical Western movie. Jeffries jumped at the chance to star as the crooning buckaroo Jeff Kincaid in *Harlem on the Prairie*, released in 1938. The dashing baritone sang five numbers in the film, backed on some by the vocal groups the Four Tones and the Four Blackbirds. The movie was filmed on location near Victorville, California, at the African-American dude ranch of one N. B. Murray. The film had a standard-issue singing Western plot—cowboy meets girl; outlaws kill girl's father; cowboy fulfills father's wishes, defeating outlaws in the process; girl goes off with cowboy. But audiences liked it, and the press gave it favorable notices, particularly Jeffries's renditions of the title song and his "swing version of 'Old Folks at Home,'" according to the *New York Amsterdam News.* The film premiered at Harlem's famed Apollo Theatre before moving to a Broadway movie palace, the first black Western to do so.

Harlem on the Prairie set the standard for other Jeffries vehicles, also filmed at the Murray ranch. His sophomore effort, *The Bronze Buckaroo* (which was to become Jeffries's nickname), introduced Bob Blake, the singing cowboy— Jeffries's character for the next few movies, along with sidekick Dusty (played in each by Lucius Brooks). The Four Tones also reappeared, in the 1939 films *Harlem Rides the Range* and *Two Gun Man from Harlem*. The plot of the latter was slightly more intricate, with Blake escaping the range for New York City after being wrongly accused of murder. Taking on the identity of Harlem gangster Deacon, he returns west, solves the crime, redeems himself, removes his disguise, and gets the girl.

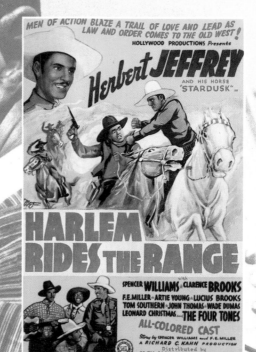

By 1940 the Bronze Buckaroo films had run their course. Jeffries toured with the Four Tones, then joined Duke Ellington's orchestra as a featured vocalist. His biggest Ellington hit was the 1941 recording "Flamingo," which led to Jeffries getting his own contract with Columbia, then Mercury. In the 1950s, Jeffries became a popular performer on the French Riviera—not far from the Camargue region of France, where French cowboys still round up wild horses. Today, Jeffries makes his home in Palm Springs and occasionally performs at Western music gatherings.

Jeffries certainly helped to pave the way for black actors to play cowboys in movies, but only after the Civil Rights Movement of the 1960s did things really improve with serious roles opening up for African-Americans. A few early examples are *100 Rifles*, starring football star Jim Brown, and the Sidney Poitier–Harry Belafonte film *Buck and the Preacher*. The 1965 Western spoof *Cat Ballou*, starring Jane Fonda and Lee Marvin, featured Nat King Cole in his last film role as a roving troubadour with partner Stubby Kaye. Mario van Peebles made real headway presenting strong black characters in the 1993 film *Posse*, which he directed and starred in. For Peebles, it was important to make a "historically accurate movie that recalled the multicultural nature of the Old West." And in so doing, he put a dent in one of the greatest myths of the cowboy perpetrated by Hollywood over the past eight decades.

Nat "King" Cole (above), impossibly smooth for his role as roving minstrel in the smart 1960s spoof *Cat Ballou*. A veteran of jazz legend Earl Hines's band, Herb Jeffries—incorrectly billed here as Jeffrey (inset)—gave a black face to the singing cowboy. Now in his nineties, he is still active today, making appearances at Western music and film gatherings. Mario van Peebles directed and starred in *Posse* (1993), a view of the west—particularly the southern West—seen through angry black eyes (following pages).

Wild Bill Elliott, aka Red Ryder, righted wrongs and overcame evil in the popular 1940s series from Republic Pictures. His horse Thunder was reputedly the fastest in the West. George O'Brien and Laraine Day are shown in the background (opposite) in *The Painted Desert* (1938). A B-movie buff's B-movie, it had the same name as an earlier B-movie (1931) starring William Boyd (before he played Hopalong Cassidy), and even contains scenes shot for the like-titled predecessor.

Killer B's
HOPPY AND HORSE OPERAS
TO THE RESCUE

FROM 1935 TO 1954, ACTION-DRIVEN B-WESTERNS PROLIFERATED IN HOLLYWOOD. SUCH FILMS BECAME THE BREAD AND BUTTER FOR LEADING MEN, INCLUDING WILLIAM BOYD, CHARLES STARRETT, BILL ELLIOTT, BOB STEELE, JOHNNY MACK BROWN, TIM HOLT, AND ROCKY LANE, AS WELL AS A SLEW OF STUNTMEN AND CHARACTER ACTORS.

While continuing to propagate myths of the West, these oaters also reflected the American character in their themes and plots. With twenty years of filmmaking experience, Hollywood had developed an assembly-line system for Western movies that was economical and quick. Recycling was key: the contract player system, structure, plots, and locations established in the 1920s formed the basis for what was to come. Previously shot footage of posses and outlaws galloping across a desert or of a stagecoach plummeting over a cliff could be used again and again. Throughout the 1930s, Ken Maynard, Hoot Gibson, Harry Carey, Tim McCoy, and Buck Jones would star in series Westerns, though they began to lose steam at the box office as they aged and a new generation of actors emerged. Eventually, they played supporting roles or teamed up in pictures.

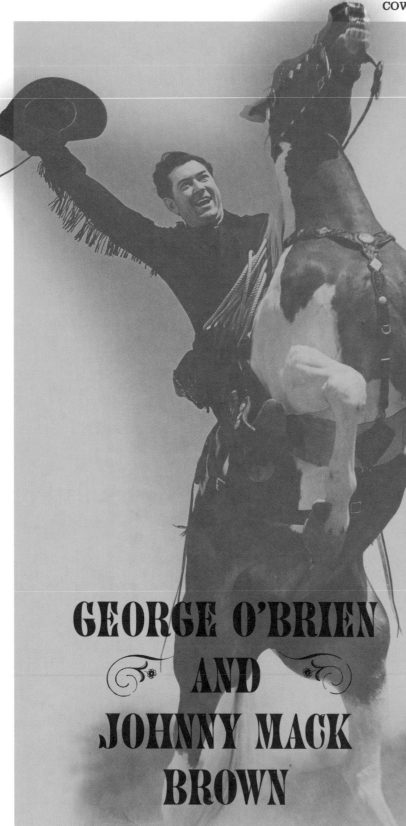

GEORGE O'BRIEN AND JOHNNY MACK BROWN

Some actors who had starred in silent films emerged as kings of B-Westerns in the 1930s. The athletic and personable George O'Brien, born in San Francisco in 1900, met Tom Mix in 1919 and became his assistant cameraman for two years. Director Lambert Hillyer then hired O'Brien as a bit player and stuntman, which led to his audition for John Ford's *The Iron Horse*. His role as the cowboy Davy brought him stardom in 1924, which led to roles in other types of films. He never strayed far from the sagebrush, however, and in the 1930s devoted himself exclusively to Westerns. He was Fox's top cowboy star in a series of Zane Grey classics, including the 1931 remake of *Riders of the Purple Sage*. The old West mixed with the new in some O'Brien pictures, including *The Cowboy Millionaire* (1935), in which he plays a dude ranch Romeo who travels from Arizona to London to catch the crooks and get the girl. The film was such a crowd pleaser that it was "novelized" in book form as part of the Big Little Book series.

O'Brien moved from Fox to RKO later in the decade, as Fox eased out of making Westerns. His films such as *Lawless Valley* "were more popular with adults than most B's," according to film historian William Everson, "not only because he could act, or because he was remembered with affection from the 1920s, but also because his light touch with humor never failed to please." O'Brien left the movies to serve in World War II but returned to play bit parts in a few John Ford Westerns before retiring.

Like O'Brien, Johnny Mack Brown had found earlier success in larger-scale movies before moving into B's. The Alabama-born college football star played opposite Greta Garbo, Mary Pickford, and Joan Crawford in romantic dramas. His first Western lead was in *Billy the Kid* (1930), coached by Bill Hart and directed by King Vidor. His career then foundered, and in 1935 he started acting in a series of low-budget oaters. With his Southern drawl and dark good looks, Brown regained popularity as a kind of gentlemanly cowboy in a 1939–41 series for Universal and then Monogram. Over the course of a number of six-reelers, he worked with two different types of sidekick, one played by crusty character actor Raymond Hatton, the other by goofy Fuzzy Knight. Both served as the studly he-man's foil: Knight would get into some sort of scrape, from which Brown would rescue him, and Hatton would offer an older man's counsel and experience in righting wrongs.

HOPALONG CASSIDY

One of the biggest Western stars to emerge in the 1930s was William Boyd, born in Ohio in 1898. He had been a 1920s matinee idol in films directed by Cecil B. DeMille and others, but by the early 1930s, Boyd's career had bottomed out. In 1931, newspapers had mistakenly run his picture when another actor named William Boyd got busted for public intoxication; this cost him his reputation in Hollywood. When the phone stopped ringing, Boyd hit the bottle. His redemption came by way of the role with which he became identified: Hopalong Cassidy. Boyd completely redefined the character from the way Clarence Mulford described him in his Hopalong Cassidy novels. Far from a red-haired, mustachioed, hard-drinking varmint, Boyd's Cassidy was a silver-haired, good-natured father figure with a hearty, booming laugh. Working with producer Harry Sherman, Boyd acted in fifty-four Cassidy films between 1935 and 1944; in 1946, Boyd produced the series himself, making a dozen or so more, as well as purchasing the rights to the

103

Hi-Ho Flag! Johnny Mack Brown (opposite) on his stalwart mount Flag successfully negotiated the downsizing of salary and ego from main feature to B-movie hero. William Boyd (right) played Hopalong Cassidy as the oldest and kindliest gunslinger in town. The astute Boyd understood that the real money was in the merchandising and control of production.

104

Sherman films along with the rights to merchandize the name and image of Hopalong Cassidy. Moving to the infant television in 1948, he won millions of new fans, making a fortune in the process.

Unlike the heroes in most B-movies, Boyd wore a black hat and outfit. Given that he was new to Westerns in the 1930s, Boyd wasn't much of a rider, but he grew so close to his horse Topper that when the stallion died in the early 1950s, Boyd reportedly never rode again. His stunt double, Cliff Lyons, did much of the riding in the early Cassidy pictures, after Boyd fell off his horse during the first one, and broke his leg. Fortunately, his limp during filming was completely in character for Hopalong. Apparently, Boyd so identified with his new role that he gave up drinking, smoking, and womanizing, claiming that "the old Boyd no longer exists."

Right from the beginning, the Boyd–Sherman collaborations were beautifully filmed in stunning locations and featured strong casts, including Bob (Robert) Mitchum as a frequent bad guy. Cassidy didn't do a lot of fighting himself; most of that was left to his younger, starry-eyed sidekick—first Johnny Nelson, played by Jimmy Ellison, then Lucky Jenkins, played by Russell Hayden. To provide humor, George "Gabby" Hayes joined the cast from 1936 to 1940 as older codger Windy Halliday, followed by silent screen comic Andy Clyde as the garrulous California Carlson.

Hopalong and California Carson come out shooting in *Twilight on the Trail* (1941), directed by Howard Bretherton. Athos, Porthos, and Aramis (opposite) ride the range; an early permutation of the tumbleweed triumvirate included (from left) Ray Corrigan, Syd Saylor (in his lone outing as Lullaby), and Bob Livingston, seen here in *The Three Mesquiteers* (1936), directed by Ray Taylor.

Cowboy Trios

A roving trio of cowboys became a popular new device in the 1930s, an innovation that helped to keep small-town movie theaters full. The model developed by Hoppy films was similar to that of Republic's Three Mesquiteers series. It included a romantic young buck, a levelheaded handsome hero, and an older (or fatter) comical rube. The Three Mesquiteers were based on characters developed by novelist William Colt McDonald, who'd placed gringo versions of Dumas's three musketeers within a Western setting. The popular Mesquiteers series ran from 1936 to 1943, and featured twelve different actors in nine different trios in a total of

fifty-one features. The first—and arguably best—grouping included Bob Livingston (Stoney Brooke), Ray Corrigan (Tucson Smith), and Max Terhune (Lullaby Joslin); Max's ventriloquist abilities were put to use via his dummy sidekick, Elmer. The Mesquiteers, as joint owners of the 3M ranch, rode into all kinds of action-packed predicaments, which usually involved their rescuing helpless women and/or children. In *Three Texas Steers* they aid a hapless blonde leading a carnival troupe comprised of acrobats, midgets, and an obviously fake gorilla (who falls for Lullaby); in *Heart of the Rockies* they defeat unscrupulous hillbilly rustlers with a penchant for poaching wildlife on park lands. "The idea of three heroes cooperating seemed to fit the New Deal spirit of the 1930s when the nation pulled together to overcome the Depression," points out Western historian Ray White. "World War II intensified and emphasized this need for teamwork and may have helped to maintain the series' popularity." As in many horse operas, the Three Mesquiteers rode the range as Old West cowboys but often encountered contemporary problems. In *Valley of Hunted Men* (1942), for example, they defeat a gang of Nazi spies.

Other studios developed their own sagebrush trios— Twenties stars Buck Jones, Tim McCoy, and Raymond Hatton found new life teaming as the Rough Riders in a Monogram series that ran from 1941 until Jones's death. A similar grouping, composed of Ken Maynard, Hoot Gibson, and Bob Steele, became the Trail Blazers. The Range Busters, produced by Monogram in 1941, featured former Mesquiteers Corrigan and Terhune, along with singing cowboy John "Dusty" King.

Republic's Mesquiteers beat out the others in popularity. Overall, Republic was putting out the best and most successful B's in the 1930s and 1940s. "Republic got more excitement into their chases, more pep into their stunts, and more punch into their fights, than any other studio," according to William Everson. "Camera work was always clean, sharp, and crystal clear, locations first-class…and their musical scores were among the best in the business."

Young Duke Wayne wasn't too proud to take a turn in the saddle as Stoney Brooke in Republic's cash cow series featuring The Three Mesquiteers. Here he is with Ray Corrigan (as Tucson Smith) and Max Terhune (Lullaby Joslin) in *The Night Riders*.

106

NEW ANGLES ON THE WESTERN

Studios began coming up with all kinds of gimmicks to sustain interest in Westerns. Obviously, the most successful innovation was the musical Western. One concept was a Western cast entirely of "little people"— dwarves and midgets. Produced by Jed Buell, *The Terror of Tiny Town* is a truly bizarre picture that featured miniature sets and diminutive cowboys, saloon girls, and outlaws. It was never repeated. Less sensational but odd in its own way was *Rawhide* (1938), in which baseball legend Lou Gehrig starred opposite singing cowboy Smith Ballew. With constant references to baseball, the plot revolves around the player's departure from the game to run a ranch and the problems he encounters. Dressed to the nines in buckaroo gear, Gehrig cut quite a dude figure. After Ballew's crooning cowboy lawyer successfully thwarts the evil cattlemen trying to intimidate Gehrig, the athlete shucks the ranch after all when he gets a call from Florida that he's needed at spring training.

Along with such all-American heroes as Gehrig, B-Westerns featured nationalistic American values. "The simplicity of the plots, with their emphasis on the certain triumph of good over evil, revealed an optimistic frame of mind that Americans generally exhibited about life," according to Ray White. "The speed with which the B-Western hero outsmarted and dispatched the villains also expressed the American appreciation for action. These fast-paced horse operas fit what most Americans conceived to be the proper method of problem solving: do something, and do it quickly."

Lou Gehrig, the baseball-playing cowboy, shown in the movie *Rawhide* (1938). *The Terror of Tiny Town* (1938), shown in the inset, tried to turn the wide open spaces of the West into Lilliput. What were they thinking of? This desperate gimmick deservedly failed.

New Sagebrush Heroes

A popular new actor to fit that bill in the 1930s was Charles Starrett, the somewhat swarthy star of a string of B's for Columbia, starting with the aptly titled *The Gallant Defender* in 1936. A native of Massachusetts and graduate of Dartmouth, Starrett came to Westerns after stints in theater and Hollywood romantic comedies. He found his calling in horse operas, particularly the role of the Durango Kid. Long on action and short on dialogue, the Kid leaps onto his stallion and gets the job done with fists flying. Much of the leaping and other daredevil feats were in fact performed by stuntman Jock Mahoney, who later starred in the television Westerns *The Range Rider* and *Yancy Derringer*. The durable Durango Kid series had Starrett transform from mild-mannered cowhand Steve into the black-garbed, kerchief-over-the-face good badman, the Durango Kid. In *Bandits of El Dorado*, see how the Kid brings to justice a greedy

vigilante who lured hapless outlaws seeking a Mexican lair, then murdered them. Smiley Burnette provides comic relief, sometimes veering into politically incorrect humor with his hillbilly combo, the Georgia Crackers.

Another distinctive all-action hero who took on a long-running role was Gordon "Wild Bill" Elliott, known for playing Red Ryder. The Missouri native modeled himself after William S. Hart, creating a realistic, subtly played cowboy character. In contrast to his clean-cut peers Starrett and Boyd, Elliott's rounder didn't always abstain from booze or refuse to set foot in a saloon. Sometimes the rugged-looking Elliott, who got his start riding in rodeos and as an extra in early movies, even played an outlaw. Unlike most other range riders, Elliott's character wore his guns with the handles facing forward. Playing Wild Bill Hickok in a 1938 serial must have prompted

Charles Starrett (above) as the Durango Kid with Gene's and Roy's old sidekick, the hysterical Smiley Burnette, take on the baddies in *Raiders of Tomahawk Creek* (1950). The black kerchief added a frisson of glamour to the Kid's do-good reputation. By day, he was the Clark Kent of the cowpokes—mild of manner and white of hat (opposite).

Elliott to copy Hickok's style. It also netted Elliott his "Wild Bill" moniker. As in the original radio serial and Fred Harmon comic book series, Elliott's Red Ryder hung out with a young Indian protégé named Little Beaver, here featuring child actor Bobby Blake, future star of *In Cold Blood* and *Baretta*. Blake's precocious Little Beaver (with the most stilted dialogue ever), along with the local schoolmarm and her aunt, were kept out of harm's way by Ryder.

Other names among the B-Western heroes during the 1940s included Buster Crabbe, better known as Flash Gordon and Buck Rogers in the sci-fi serials of the 1930s. Mesquiteer Bob Livingston played a popular version of the Lone Ranger in the Republic serial *The Lone Ranger Rides Again*, among other roles. Bob Steele also acted in Western trio pictures, and starred in dozens of oaters as the lone hero. Specializing as the Lone Rider, George Houston had the company of Al "Fuzzy" St. John in a number of his motion pictures. The son of silent cowboy star Jack Holt, Tim Holt was one of RKO's most durable Western contract players in a long-running series who went on to play featured roles in such films as *Stagecoach* and *The Magnificent Ambersons*.

THE LAST OF THE B's

Allan "Rocky" Lane—born Harry Albershart—acted in a number of dramas before moving to Republic to star in a couple of Western serials. In 1945 he took over the Red Ryder series from Wild Bill Elliott; then, at the end of the oater food chain, he played a dark-clad buckaroo named, well, Rocky Lane. By the late 1940s, the Lane B's were so cheaply and quickly made that the recycled location scenes didn't even come close to matching the new footage shot in the studio.

Two latter-day B-stars who got stuck in similar shoestring productions had some of the more colorful stage names going. Former rodeo champ Sunset Carson couldn't act his way out of a paper bag, but between his riding skills and the minimal amount of dialogue in his pictures, who cared? As for Lash (born Alfred) LaRue, he got his nickname thanks to the whip he wielded more often than a gun. With his wavy brunette pompadour and skintight black garb, the

Louisiana-born LaRue certainly had fashion sense. Apparently, his features were so similar to Humphrey Bogart's they hurt his chances in Hollywood, but in films like *Outlaw Country* and *Law of the Lash*, LaRue was definitely his own man. "Fuzzy" St. John, the hardest-working sidekick in Hollywood, also participated in many LaRue pictures, while Smiley Burnette, the most musical—and perhaps the second busiest—sidekick in show biz, played in several Carson films to help get him started.

By the early 1950s, only a half dozen or so B-Western stars were active, as compared to some thirty a decade earlier. Most had grown older and stouter, losing their appeal as action heroes. Some continued to get work as bit players, while others ended up as character actors in television programs. Rocky Lane, for example, became the voice of Mr. Ed the talking horse.

With so many B's reedited and sold to television, the studios cut down on the production of new ones. They could make just as much money selling the oldies to TV networks as they could earn from diminished box office returns in half-empty small-town theaters. And the unreality of bullet wounds that didn't bleed or even show up didn't jibe with the experiences of shell-shocked World War II vets. The action fantasies of a

110

A poster (above) advertises *The Fighting Vigilantes* (1947), a vehicle for Lash LaRue, the dude with attitude. Allan "Rocky" Lane (opposite) is doing what all tough cowboys do when they are in a hurry, in *Rustlers on Horseback* (1950), an archetypal B-movie with a labyrinthine and tedious plot. Rocky Lane stars as undercover Marshal Rocky Lane, who infiltrates a gang of villains cunningly disguised as a bunch of harmless booksellers. Yes, really.

black-and-white world of good versus evil seemed less and less relevant in the days of the Cuban Missile Crisis and duck 'n' cover training for possible nuclear attack. The escapism provided for kids by Western matinees was also being replaced by a new kind of entertainment on jukeboxes and at sock hops; the kids' brand-new heroes—some of whom looked an awful lot like Lash LaRue—played rock and roll.

The B-Western that holds the distinction of being the last one ever made is *Two Guns and a Badge*, directed by one Lewis D. Collins and starring Johnny-come-lately Wayne Morris. Released in September 1954, it sounded the death knell for horse operas.

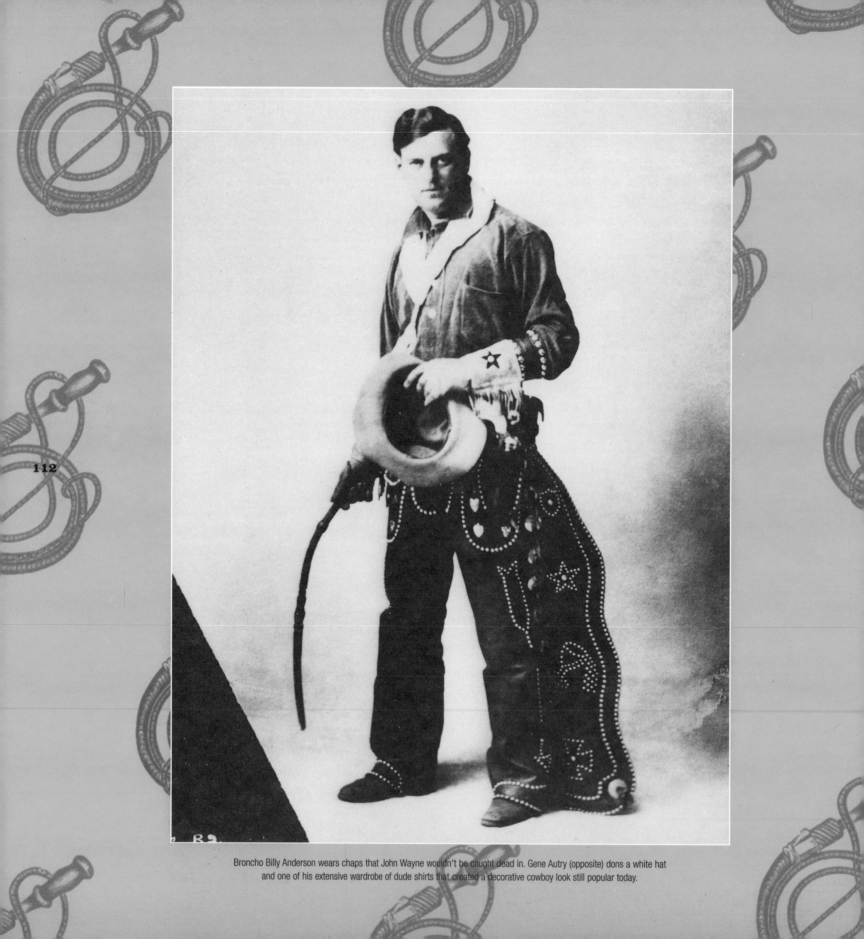

Broncho Billy Anderson wears chaps that John Wayne wouldn't be caught dead in. Gene Autry (opposite) dons a white hat and one of his extensive wardrobe of dude shirts that created a decorative cowboy look still popular today.

I Can Tell by Your Outfit
That You Are a Cowboy
THE DRESS OF WESTERN MOVIES

STETSON HAT, FLOWING NECKERCHIEF, POINTY-TOED HIGH-TOPPED BOOTS: THIS IS THE ATTIRE THAT IMMEDIATELY IDENTIFIES THE WEARER AS A COWBOY, AND THROUGH ITS APPEARANCE IN THOUSANDS OF WESTERN MOVIES WE KNOW WHAT A BUCKAROO LOOKS LIKE.

In reality, though, most celluloid cowboys exaggerated authentic elements from nineteenth-century range rider's garb, popularizing new styles to the extent that they actually changed the dress of bona fide buckaroos. Before the 1920s, few major film studios employed staff costume designers. Until then, most screen actors' wardrobes consisted of their own clothing or garments rented from theatrical costume companies. The earliest silents, like *The Great Train Robbery*, used oversized hats and bandannas so that Eastern actors would be recognized as Westerners. The first cowboy star, Broncho Billy Anderson, devised an individualized look largely inspired by Buck Taylor and other members of Buffalo Bill's cowboy retinue, and images of Westerners shown on the covers of dime novels. On his wrists, Broncho Billy wore leather cuffs adorned with a single star, and on his legs studded batwing or woolly sheepskin chaps. The former weren't worn until the 1920s and the

latter had a degree of authenticity—if you happened to be a Wyoming or Montana cowboy who needed the furry leg coverings for warmth. Most nineteenth-century cowpunchers, wore "shotgun" or "stovepipe" style leather chaps to protect the legs, and some wore the leather cuffs to shield their wrists from rope burns when wrapping a lariat around the arm for a strong grip on a testy calf.

William S. Hart did his best to look like a real Westerner, and even had his portrait painted as one by none other than Charlie Russell. Like Broncho Billy, his authentic-looking pocketless shirt was rather drab and dusty, and he often wore a waistcoat, or vest, which real cowboys preferred instead of jackets or coats since it left their arms unrestricted but provided them with pockets for tobacco, money, and possibly a watch. As well as wrist cuffs, Hart also incorporated other details from a working cowboy's wardrobe into his movie outfits, including a Mexican sash worn under his gun belt, traditionally used by vaqueros for tying the hooves of a roped steer, and a light, ranger-style hat. And, like styles of chaps,

hat styles identified a nineteenth-century cowboy's region of the country. Southwestern buckaroos opted for large brims to shield their face from the hot sun, as originated by John B. Stetson, and named the Boss of the Plains. Montana and Wyoming cowboys wore a heavier, warmer, high-crowned hat, which came to be called the Montana Peak.

Hart fastidiously studied pictures of the nineteenth-century cowboy's dress, and consulted his buddies Charles Siringo, Bat Masterson, Wyatt Earp, and sundry old cowhands. Trying his best to imitate their look, he once explained, "The real cowboy clothes are all made for utility, not for effect. Even the silk handkerchief he wears round his neck has its uses. When he's herding cattle, he doubles the handkerchief cornerwise and puts it over his face just beneath the eyes to keep the dust out of his nose and mouth. A cowboy is usually a bit of a dandy and likes a silk handkerchief because silk is soft to the face and neck. This he fastens with a valuable ring when he can afford one; when he can't he'll use a poker-chip."

Two looks polarize the West (above): the inescapable camp of the Lone Ranger's tight pants and coy mask and the true grit style of any cowboy impersonated by the Duke. Alan Ladd and Brandon de Wilde (opposite) are pictured in the seminal *Shane*.

FROM WORK CLOTHES TO SHOW CLOTHES

The movies filmed out West with real cowboys as extras and stuntmen came close to achieving accuracy with the costumes. Thomas Ince's films between 1910 and 1914 did at least show what early twentieth-century buckaroos actually wore, although some of them hailed from the Miller Bros. 101 Ranch company and had an entertainer's flair for fashion. Rodeo cowboys—and cowgirls—had already adopted some flashy decorative motifs on their shirtfronts, following the example set by Buffalo Bill. They donned ornate outfits for fancy shooting demonstrations and rodeo parades, rather than for bronco busting or bull-dogging. Buffalo Bill and other showmen popularized fringed buckskin shirts and jackets, an elaboration of the garments that had been worn by mountain men and Plains Indians. Originally, a long fringe had been a means of shooing away insects and helping to drain rainwater off the clothing; if necessary, it could be torn off to use as a makeshift cord. Fringed buckskin appeared on many celluloid cowboys over the years, perhaps most famously in *Shane* (1953), as worn by Alan Ladd and symbolizing his gunfighter past. When Shane replaces his buckskins with woolen pants and plaid work shirt to become a farmhand, his virility is diminished; when he needs to resurrect his tough outer shell for a showdown with Jack Palance's gunslinger, the skins go back on.

Those authentic cowpunchers who worked in silent Westerns soon discovered that though the directors wanted legitimate cowboys who could ride, fight, and fall off a horse, they already had a set idea of what a buckaroo should look like and expected cowboys to dress that way. And though many a rumpled cowhand scoffed at the neater, more "streamlined" appearance of movie cowboys, they soon followed the old adage, "if you can't beat 'em, join 'em." Bit player Al Hoxie, ranch-hand brother of silent star Jack Hoxie, once recalled, "I don't think any of the boys liked to be dressed up.... You just had to dress that way in order to get by." It became expensive for cowboys to provide these flashier outfits, too. To meet their needs, the West's oldest boot and saddlery shop, Fursnows of Miles City, Montana, opened a branch in Hollywood; some of their "drugstore cowboy" goods included bright orange angora chaps, which cost upward of $40, Stetson hats at $45 and up, and Justin boots averaging around $40.

Washington-born stuntman Yakima Canutt, a rodeo champ in 1914 before he worked in early Westerns, admitted, "When I first came into the picture business, it was hard to take. They did everything the wrong way.... But after being in the picture business for some time, I began to learn that by putting showmanship into it, you're making entertainment. You can't be too authentic. You've got to add things to it to pep it up.... In my rodeo days, we feathered it up a little bit. I went into white riding trousers and two-tone shirts. I used to get some terrible write-ups: 'Who ever heard of a cowboy wearing white pants?' That kind of stuff. But it was rodeo and it was flash and we were building the game up."

115

BEAU BRUMMELS OF THE WEST

No one added as much showmanship to early Westerns as Tom Mix, the Beau Brummel of the West. At the height of his career in 1925, he reportedly toured with an entire baggage car devoted to his wardrobe. That same year, Mix was contracted by John B. Stetson to endorse his signature five-inch brim, seven-inch crown hat, which popularized and inspired the phrase "ten-gallon hat." With such influences as the Wild West show's costumery coming to the fore in his wardrobe, Mix made no pretense of showing the West as it was. The bigger a star he became, the more outrageous his outfits. Mix's success ensured that the silent screen cowboy would never again wear the clothes of the humble cowpuncher.

Thanks to Mix, many new Western styles were born. He popularized the pointed-yoke Western shirt with long multi-button cuffs and arrowhead-stitched smile pockets (front shirt pockets shaped like smiles), for the first time appearing in this costume in *Teeth* (1924). In *The Texan*, he donned a white shirt with five-button cuffs and smile pockets, gambler-striped pants tucked into cowboy boots, a ten-gallon hat, gun belt, and fringed leather gloves, or gauntlets, like those worn by Buffalo Bill. Not too many screen cowboys took up the gauntlets. A definitive Mix style appeared in his adaptation of Zane Grey's *Riders of the Purple Sage*: a black shirt with white piped pointed yokes, smile pockets with embroidered arrowheads, and long cuffs; a loosely tied silk muffler; and tight black riding breeches with a double seat outlined in white. For public appearances, Mix often dressed in a gleaming white jacket with matching riding pants, adorned with contrasting color piping. He favored leather straps with silver buckles running down the leg of the pants from knee to ankle. Another Mix favorite was a cream-colored shirt with a bib front, embroidered with red roses. One Mix confidant claimed the star did his own embroidery. Whatever the case, Mix was the first film star to decorate his shirts with a floral motif, a look earlier adopted by Buffalo Bill—and before him by Napoleon and other European royals.

Tom Mix shows us how to team flappy chaps, an embroidered bibfront shirt, Mickey Mouse gloves, and a rope—and still look hard. Mix (opposite) wears a rather more streamlined outfit for close work in an ambush situation in *Riders of the Purple Sage*.

Silent movie stars following in Mix's wake gussied themselves up a bit but couldn't come close to him—though many tried, particularly with oversized Stetsons. Most silent movie stars favored a particular signature hat style, with a unique crease in the crown. With the proliferation of the Montana Peak hat during the 1920s, the individual regional styles vanished, as working cowhands actually adopted the look of the screen stars. The same thing happened with other items of the cowboys' "rig," or outfit. Batwing chaps, which were unheard of before the 1920s, became the norm for celluloid buckaroos, even when they were playing nineteenth-century cattlepunchers. Soon, cowpokes and rodeo riders all over the country followed suit.

Mix also popularized "branding" one's rig. He put his trademark TM motif on everything he wore, right down to his underwear, and adopted a straight shooter logo. Horse-lover Buck Jones used the horseshoe as his symbol, and had it embroidered on his shirt collars. Seemingly decorative details could serve more practical purposes: Ken Maynard wore frontier trousers with buckled straps along the side, as well as stirrups at the bottom, to prevent the pant legs from coming out of his boots while riding.

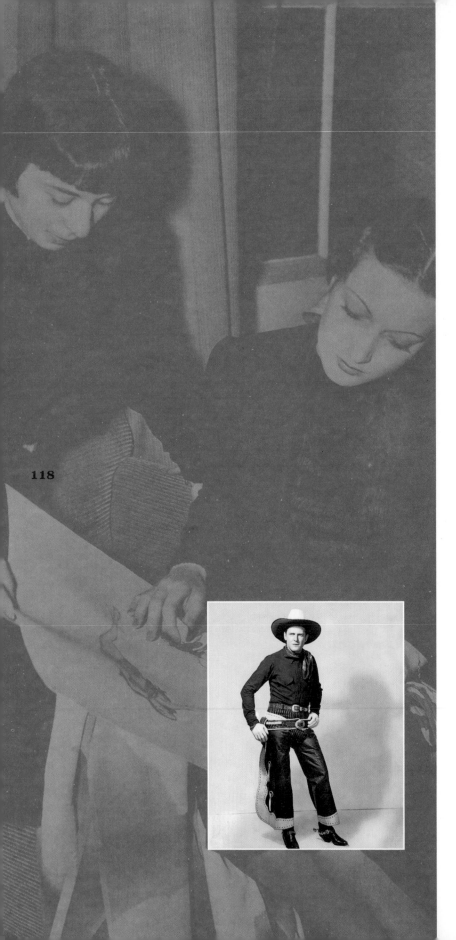

The extravagant buckaroo style taken up by B-Western stars flourished into the 1930s. Another development was the symbolic use of black and white to differentiate the good guys from the bad. For the most part, God-fearing buckaroos wore white hats, added white elements to their clothing, and often rode a white horse. Frequently sporting a mustache, outlaws took themselves seriously as princes of darkness, donning black hats, black clothes, and galloping along on black horses. An exception to this "rule" was the Good Samaritan Hopalong Cassidy, who wore a dashing black outfit with matching black hat, but perhaps this choice was to contrast with actor William Boyd's glistening silver hair and his white steed Topper. The only other white item Cassidy displayed was a distinctive clasp on his scarf, crafted out of a bone from a bull's spine.

Some movies parodied fancy costumes by presenting outlandish-looking outfits on buffoonish cowpokes or Eastern dudes. An early example is humorist Will Rogers's *Doubling for Romeo* (1921): his protagonist Sam the cowhand gets duded up by his bunkhouse pals so he can make it in the movies. His buddies give him a pair of over-the-top angora chaps, a lavishly decorated shirt, fringed wrist cuffs, and embroidered vest. When they present him with an enormous ten-gallon hat, they offer, "Here's a thing that was originally used for a tent. It's the nearest we could get to the one Tom Mix wears." When handed a giant neckerchief, Sam inquires, "What's this—a bedspread?" Once he's gussied up, his buddies wonder, "How's the poor feller gonna get on his horse with all those trimmins' on?"

Edith Head (shown in background) was one of Hollywood's legendary costume designers. Ken Maynard, a stunt cowboy, models some chaps that surely should be saved for Sunday Best in the inset. Gene Autry's slick black shirt and white neckerchief (opposite) puts his sartorially challenged colleagues to shame in *Public Cowboy No. 1* (1937).

Peacocks of a Feather Flocking Together

Resplendent finery reached its peak with the singing cowboys, beginning with Gene Autry and continuing through to Rex Allen, the last of the singing cowboys, who went so far as wearing rhinestone-fringed gold lamé outfits. Obviously inspired by Tom Mix, Autry donned tight pants tucked into decorative boots with fancy Western shirts decorated with piping and embroidery. His signature style was a black shirt with contrasting white piping and lacing. He also favored thunderbird embroidered motifs on his shirt yokes. Following suit, Roy Rogers went in for even more ornate attire, going for fringe, giant embroidered portraits of his dog Bullet, and—for live performances—rhinestones. Rogers's pictures fared less well with the critics than Autry's because of what movie historian Don Miller calls the "era of the shrieking Rogers costumery, stretching the willing suspension of disbelief to the breaking point." Interestingly, as the shirts, pants, and boots got fancier on singing cowboys, the hats got smaller, with the Montana Peak style gradually disappearing. In its place were lower-crowned, smaller-brimmed Stetsons, followed by the Resistol brand.

Where did Autry, Rogers, Allen, and their dressed-up singing cowboy companions get such duds? A trio of Jewish tailors of Eastern-European origin were responsible for creating the look. Nathan Turk (born Teig) and Rodeo Ben (born Bernard Lichtenstein) both immigrated from Poland after the turn of the century. Nudie Cohn was born Nutya Kotlyrenko in Kiev, Russia. All three tailors adapted embroidery motifs and sewing techniques from their native homelands, merging them with the decorative style of the Mexican vaqueros and adding a dash of down-home American buckaroo. The resulting fantastical outfits they produced were quite unparalleled in their singularity—and in their highly refined tailoring. A feast for the eyes, the garments were also extremely well made, designed to withstand the rigors of vigorous action scenes as well as arduous performances in front of audiences.

In the 1920s Turk and Rodeo Ben opened their custom shops in the San Fernando Valley and

Philadelphia respectively, catering first to rodeo riders and then to celluloid cowboys, including regulars Gene Autry and Roy Rogers. Autry and Rogers, in fact, both posed for Rodeo Ben's mail-order catalogs. Nudie, who had up till then been manufacturing skimpy, spangly costumes for burlesque stars in

New York, moved into Western wear after relocating to California in the 1940s. His first clients were Western music performers in 1949; but by the time he opened a shop in North Hollywood in 1951 his clientele had expanded to include every big name in Westerns. His star-studded shop became

a hangout where you could always count on bumping into such luminaries as Monte Hale, Gene Autry, Roy Rogers, Rex Allen, or John Wayne. Turk and Nudie both did commissions for studio costume designers such as Edith Head, the top designer for Paramount from the 1920s right up to the late 1960s. Head designed the costume for Boyd's first Hoppy film, as well as outfitting other notable Western stars, including John Wayne, Gary Cooper, and, later, Robert Redford and Paul Newman. According to her autobiography, she often rented entire wardrobes for "B pictures and horse operas" from Western Costume, which was started by a colleague of Bill Hart's who'd originally been an Indian trader. Another friend of Hart's, Joe de Yong, was one of Hollywood's early costume designers and illustrators. Hart had met de Yong through the illustrator Charlie Russell. De Yong's first stint in Hollywood was costuming Cecil B. DeMille's *The Plainsman* (1936), starring Gary Cooper and Jean Arthur in the roles of Wild Bill Hickok and Calamity Jane. Other studio designers who outfitted Westerns included Howard Greer at Famous Players-Lasky, Travis Banton at Paramount, and Adrian at MGM Studios.

Etta Place (Katharine Ross), Butch Cassidy (Paul Newman), and Sundance (Robert Redford) (above) try to pass themselves off as upstanding citizens visiting a New York City photographer in a scene from *Butch Cassidy and the Sundance Kid* (1969). Autry (opposite) models another of the hundreds of shirts he had custom-made by Rodeo Ben, Turk, and Nudie, beginning in the 1930s.

COWGIRLS

For the most part, women in Westerns wore whatever fashion was stylish when the movie was made, lending even more implausibility to their roles. In 1930's *Cimarron*, for example, Richard Dix as Yancey Cravat always looked every inch the Westerner, while his wife Sabra (Irene Dunne) made a point of wearing and showing off the latest Eastern fashions for the ladies' auxiliary. Adding a bit of sex appeal, saloon-hall girls in Westerns wore as little as they could get away with, somewhat modeled after Parisian cancan girls with frilly petty pants. After Howard Hughes's spicy, and at the time controversial, Billy the Kid film *The Outlaw* (made in 1943 but not released until 1950), starring Jane Russell as Rio, the Kid's main squeeze, women wore skintight, low-cut outfits, showing off heaving cleavage and shapely legs.

123

From the earliest films, though, there were cowgirls who wore what their rodeo-riding counterparts did: fringed split skirts, bolero vests, fancy boots, and large-brimmed hats. Queen of the West Dale Evans became a Nudie regular. She collaborated with Nudie on some of her decorative ensembles, many of which coordinated with those of her husband. She always wore her large-brimmed hat cocked on the back of her head so that it framed her lovely face like a halo. The Texas-born Evans once commented that she got lots of grief for it from "real" cowgals and guys— who wore a hat pulled snugly down over their forehead so it wouldn't fly off.

Dressed to kill, Jane Russell steams in *The Outlaw*, wearing a costume that no self-respecting cowgirl would wear to bed. This was an improbable tale of Pat Garrett, Billy the Kid, Doc Holliday, and the Doc's woman, Rio (Russell), who eventually falls for the Kid. It was billed as the picture that couldn't be stopped.

124

THE RETURN OF REALISM

Many film historians point to Howard Hawks's *Red River* (1948), with its fairly accurate portrayal of the first cattle drive to Abilene, as a return to realistic costumery. Its star, John Wayne, influenced by Harry Carey and John Ford, had dressed mostly in no-nonsense cowhand garb since his start in pictures in the 1920s. He could usually be found in a bib-front shirt, which historically dated to Civil War days, and Levi's, which most cowboys didn't actually wear until the 1920s (before that, they wore woolen trousers), with folded-up cuffs of several inches. Cowhands sometimes stashed cigarettes and cash in their cuffs. Wayne's typically beige hat changed size over the years. In *Stagecoach* (1939), Wayne's Ringo Kid wore suspenders—and for good reason: belt loops on trousers were a twentieth-century fashion innovation.

According to the actor's son, Michael, his father used to help the costume department turn his garments into realistic-looking duds. On family trips to Catalina Island, before shooting a new movie, Wayne would enlist the help of his kids to wad up his movie clothes, tie them with ropes, and throw them into the ocean, attached by rope to the pier. After three days, they'd haul them in—beat up to the point where they could pass for a hard-riding buckaroo's garb. On Wayne's John Ford films, he'd be provided with eight versions of the same shirt and pants—all with varying degrees of abuse to realistically depict the wear and tear of the trail. Costume designers used mineral oil to stain felt

cowboy hats with "sweat." To add "distress" to the clothing, wardrobe personnel used sandpaper, fuller's earth, and sometimes even blowtorches.

Surpassing even Wayne's rough 'n' tumble look was that of the Sergio Leone "spaghetti Westerns" of the 1960s. Star Clint Eastwood looked down and dirty in his flat-crowned hat, Mexican-style serape or poncho, and flared trousers, which helped to influence the "antistyle" of cosmic cowboy hippies later in the decade.

A fashion statement that became widely popular in the 1980s was the flowing canvas overcoat known as the duster. Though some rubber "fish brand" slickers had been worn by turn-of-the-century ranchers, the style was actually native to Australia. It first started showing up cinematically in *Red River* (1948), though unlike its historical predecessor it was not

split up the back to facilitate riding nor did it have extra fabric to compensate for the saddle pommel. This inaccurate, movie-concocted duster was seen again in Ford's *The Searchers* (1956) and Sam Peckinpah's *The Wild Bunch* (1969), which linked the coat to outlaws. It became firmly associated with bad boys, thanks to *The Long Riders* (1980), when it was worn by the Younger brothers and Jesse and Frank James. Three years on, the seven identically dressed deputies who wore light-colored dusters in *Pale Rider* took the coat back to the good guys. By then, this fashion statement created by Westerns was also being worn by cowboys, dudes, and wannabes all over America. Every few years, when the cowboy looms large again—as happened when *Lonesome Dove* became a hit on television, creating a craze for the "Gus hat," which was another name for the Montana Peak—cowboys continue to influence the dress not only of the West, but of the world.

In *Red River* (1948), John Wayne (opposite) actually looked like he had just ridden herd from Texas to Abilene, and so did his clothes. This costuming set the style for more realistic Western dress. Realism gave way to style (above) in Walter Hill's *The Long Riders* (1980), which saw the James and Younger gangs garbed in the impractical but cool long coats known as dusters.

The King of the Cowboys comes to grips with a Tootsie Roll, one of the many products wholeheartedly endorsed by Roy Rogers and Dale Evans. "Cowboys and Injuns" became the only game in town (opposite) from the 1940s onward, when toy guns helped to hone the trigger fingers of junior shootists everywhere.

Western Treasures
THE MARKETING OF THE COWBOY IMAGE

AS SOON AS COWBOYS CAUGHT THE PUBLIC'S FANCY, THE BUCKAROO IMAGE WAS USED TO SELL MERCHANDISE. AS WELL AS MOVING PRODUCTS, THIS USE ALSO SERVED TO BROADEN THE MYTHOLOGICAL IDEAL OF THE HEROIC PRINCES OF THE PLAINS.

Beginning in the 1870s, buckaroo images decorated everyday items. With the popularity of Buffalo Bill's Wild West show, Cody's visage appeared on products and souvenirs. And in the wake of Tom Mix came thousands of products endorsed by celluloid cowboys, sustaining and continuing to spread the idea of the West to future generations.

In the nineteenth century, household items ranging from spools of thread and shaving razors to laxatives, buckets of lard, and comestibles like prunes, corn, breakfast cereal, and peaches were distributed in packaging bearing the noble visage of the cowboy, sometimes astride his bucking bronco. Home furnishings and accessories, including serving trays, toy banks, and even a Steinway piano, displayed Western scenes. Certain vices associated with cowpunchers—alcohol and tobacco—frequently came to be packaged in buckaroo-adorned containers.

128

Buffalo Bill

The endorsement of products by Western entertainers began a trend that continues today. It started with William F. Cody. Buffalo Bill hired as his press agent "Arizona John" M. Burke. Burke helped Cody to develop a line of souvenirs available at his Wild West shows, and to determine which manufacturers could have the right to stamp Cody's name on their products. Along with programs, cabinet card (mounted) photographs, pennants, and posters, there were games, toys, calendars, and commemorative plates and silver.

Buffalo Bill also endorsed a line of cigars and plug tobacco and, for storing smoking supplies, a sculpted metal cigar and match holder that featured Cody seated and holding his Winchester. In 1896 the New York game makers McLoughlin Brothers created "The Wild West Game." Two years later, in 1898, the well-known Parker Brothers company of Salem, Massachusetts, began manufacturing "The Game of Buffalo Bill." Kids could get Buffalo Bill books and "Buffalo Bill's Wild West Panorama for Children," which could be folded open to reveal several scenes from the Wild West show, as well as Buffalo Bill's adventures in the West. And of course, there were children's Buffalo Bill costumes, too.

Older consumers could try to look like Buffalo Bill too, with detachable beards, mustaches, and wigs, as well as Cody's personal Stetson. One advertisement of 1900 for Stetson read: "Years ago we made specially

Buffalo Bill was the original buckaroo marketeer. No single aspect of life on the range was left unexploited; even so, William Cody was not a successful businessman and lost several fortunes.

for Colonel Cody, the 'Buffalo Bill,' a soft hat of quite tremendous proportions. This style has been adopted and worn ever since by him and many of his Western companions. Outdoor life is hard on hats, and the continued patronage of these men is a strong endorsement of the satisfaction and wonderful wear that go with every 'Stetson.' " And to clean their saddle and boots, riders could use Buffalo Bill saddle soap.

Gun manufacturers too sought out Cody's endorsement. As one Colt advertisement crowed: "Colt Revolvers have been adopted by the United States Army and Navy, the Police, Militia, and are used by Buffalo Bill's Wild West Show. They Are the Best." Cody apparently agreed, as the advertisement continued with his endorsement: "A friend gave me a 10 shot Savage Automatic Pistol for Christmas. It is the first automatic I ever owned or fired. I had turned them down without trial, and stuck to an old army revolver. Today I took the old revolver and the Savage Automatic out and fired each fifty times making, to my surprise, a much better score with the automatic than I could with my old pet gun." If Cody's testimonial wasn't enough to convince consumers, the same ad followed with the fact that "the world's crack shots, like Col. Cody, 'Bat' Masterson and Dr. Carver, say it beats any revolver.... Write to-day for 'The Tenderfoot's Turn,' a fascinating book (free) about famous crack shots, by 'Bat' Masterson."

Cody really did swear by the Winchester, however, particularly the Model 1895 rifle, and was paid to let his spectators know, with posters on display at performances announcing "Winchester Guns and Ammunition Used Exclusively by Buffalo Bill and the Wild West Show." Cody called his favorite sporting and frontier rifle "the Boss."

Buffalo Bill.

24985 This is a new departure in wooden toys and is decidedly novel in every respect. It illustrates vividly how Buffalo Bill and his scouts overcame a party of ambuscaded Indians. Best thing out. Price........................ $0.75

COLT REVOLVERS HAVE BEEN ADOPTED BY THE UNITED STATES ARMY AND NAVY, THE POLICE, MILITIA, AND ARE USED BY BUFFALO BILL'S WILD WEST SHOW.

129

TOM MIX AND TOYS GALORE

Walt Disney's Mickey Mouse initiated a boom in licensing products with a program developed by Disney's Kay Kamen to put Mickey's image and endorsement on numerous items. It was only natural that beloved cowboy heroes would follow suit, particularly the flamboyant and popular Tom Mix. The modern era of cowboy star endorsement began in a big way in the 1930s with Mix, who endorsed toys, Ralston Purina cereals (sponsors of the extremely popular Tom Mix national radio show), and of course the Tom Mix Stetson. He also endorsed some ready-made fancy shirts by Western-wear manufacturers that had started production thanks to the boom in Westerns and the resulting popularity in cowboy clothes. By the mid-1930s, kids had lots of Tom Mix items to choose from, including rings, wooden guns, and other small toys that could be ordered as premiums by listening to his radio show. Each program opened with an endorsement jingle by Tom (with Tony whinnying in the background) for yummy Ralston: "Shredded Ralston for your breakfast/ starts the day off shining bright/gives you lots of cowboy energy/with a flavor that's just right/It's

delicious and nutritious/Bite size and ready to eat/Take a tip from Tom/Go and tell your Mom/Shredded Ralston can't be beat!"

Kids could be snappy dressers like Tom by sending away Ralston cereal box tops for a leather and cloth vest with matching chaps decorated with the Tom Mix brand, as well as leather wrist cuffs with Mix's Straight Shooters logo. A typical radio ad coaxed kids to eat their cereal and reap the rewards: "Boys! Girls! I'll send you my Horseshoe Nail Ring free! For two Ralston box tops or one Ralston box top and ten cents in coin." Among other Tom Mix products were bandannas, paper dolls, boots, charm bracelets, a magnifying glass/compass, and Straight Shooter stationery. A Straight Shooter manual featured a listing of all the Tom Mix goods available, as well as the "Tom Mix Chart of Wounds." Each of the injuries he incurred as a daredevil rodeo rider, movie star, and circus performer was pointed out anatomically, including his twelve bullet wounds and forty-seven fractured bones. After Mix died from a broken neck in a 1940 car accident, commemorative items followed, including Tom Mix neckerchiefs and ties.

Most of Tom Mix's peers did not benefit as much from product endorsements or licensing deals. Several cowboy stars were featured on the lids of ice-cream containers, including Tim McCoy on Sunfreze by Arden Farms and Buck Jones, Hoot Gibson, and Ken Maynard on the Dixie Cup brand. All were featured on penny postcards available in arcade vending machines. The dime-novel tradition—albeit very much cleaned up and wholesome with no blood 'n' guts—was continued for kids via comic books and series such as the Big Little Books, published by Whitman. Mix was the most popular subject, but volumes were also available on McCoy, Jones, and Maynard. Jones, who had a 1937 kiddie radio show called *Hoofbeats*, dabbled quite extensively in an array of endorsed products for adults and children. His listeners, who belonged to his Buck Jones Rangers organization, could order a sheriff badge or his trademark horseshoe on a pin or ring. In addition to an elaborate faux pony skin outfit for kids, Jones also had his own line of Western men's shirts, as well as bandannas, boots, and hats, available through mail-order catalogs.

Cowboy dogs and horses also benefited from the endorsement craze, particularly Rin-Tin-Tin. The Westernized German shepherd was almost as popular as his heroic human counterparts, thanks to his 1920s silent movies made by Warner Bros. Ken-L-Ration dog food offered as a premium a photo of Rinty, and Ken-L-Biskets doggie snacks featured the shepherd's gallant face on the box. Later in the 1950s, Rin-Tin-Tin got his own TV show, which resulted in Rinty books, puzzles, and games. Other canine cowpokes included Strongheart the Wonder Dog, Dynamite, and Peter the Great.

131

Radio gave some cowboy heroes their start before they moved into serials or program Westerns and television. Most prominent among them were the masked Lone Ranger with his horse Silver and Indian cohort Tonto (beginning in 1933) and Red Ryder with his pint-sized Indian pal Little Beaver (1942). One junior cowpoke role model was Bobby Benson, who hailed from the H-Bar-O Ranch (for H-O Oats, sponsors of *Bobby Benson's Adventures* radio show). Each radio series came with its own gizmos, costumes, and books, many available as premiums through various bread and cereal sponsors.

"Mama, don't let your babies grow up to be cowboys," Willie Nelson and Waylon Jennings sang in vain, as kids from Texas to Connecticut threw themselves enthusiastically into the cowboy craze (opposite). Omniscient Western canine Rin-Tin-Tin, a hero in movies and his own TV show, also endorsed products from dog food to jigsaw puzzles. The dog's owner successfully played the market.

SINGING COWBOYS & MUCHO MERCHANDISE

"Dale and I are very proud of every product that bears our name."

Endorsed goods were taken to even greater heights in the following decades by Gene Autry and Roy Rogers. Starting with his success in the early 1930s as a radio and recording star, Gene Autry began putting his name and image on various products. His Gene Autry guitar came with a songbook and was available through the Sears catalog, the source for Autry's first guitar as a child. When he became Hollywood's premier singing cowboy, a bonanza of endorsed products was launched: wristwatches; toys of all kinds; kids' clothing, including cowboy suits, boots, galoshes, neckerchiefs, and pajamas; lunchboxes; books; comic books; paper dolls; and a Gene Autry bicycle. Tie-ins with Quaker Oats, Pillsbury, and Sunbeam bread led to premiums galore featuring Gene, his Melody Ranch, and his horse Champion—which had its own line of toys and books. Autry's long-running *Melody Ranch* radio show, traveling Western performances, and television program helped to extend the life span of Autry endorsement possibilities even after his movie career had peaked. An impressive collection of Autry products—along with those endorsed by other celebrity cowpokes—can be seen at the Autry Museum of Western Heritage in Los Angeles and the Gene Autry Oklahoma Museum of Local History in Gene Autry, Oklahoma.

Roy Rogers broadened the range of products still further as his popularity among children surpassed Autry's. Beginning in 1943, Roy's smiling face began gracing an array of items, from boxes of Post Cereal to cap guns, bedspreads, and alarm clocks. Once he and Dale Evans became a team, her smile could be found on a cornucopia of wares too. Eventually, more than 450 products—including children's clothing, toys, books, furnishings, and items like flashlights, binoculars, and lunchboxes—were endorsed by Roy Rogers and Dale Evans. Each

Gene Autry was a merchandiser's dream as late as the 1950s. Here he is discussing range fashions with a young fan in 1951. But his marketing star was gradually eclipsed by the double-barreled selling power of Roy Rogers and Dale Evans, shown in the inset, who rapidly established their home on an impressively wide product range.

132

endorsed item had to pass the Rogers family test; in fact, each bore a tag with the following pledge: "Dale and I are very proud of every product that bears our name, and we use these items for our own children. You pay no premium for our name. Rather, it is your assurance of authenticity and quality."

In the late 1940s and early 1950s, most American kids probably had at least one Roy Rogers product. The line included items emblazoned with the image of Trigger, Bullet the wonder dog, even Nellybelle the jeep—from Roy and Dale's TV show in the 1950s. In the 1940s, Roy Rogers was second only to Disney in the number of licensed goods. Products could be ordered through the mail by sending in cereal box tops with a little change, purchased in toy stores, or located on display in a special Roy Rogers Corral section of Sears stores. By the mid-1950s, estimates of the value of the Roy Rogers licensing brand range from $33 to $50 million. Many of these products are on display at the Roy Rogers/Dale Evans Museum in Victorville, California. Among the exhibits are a

Where Tom Mix blazed a trail across the prairie wheat (in the form of cereal), Roy Rogers followed, endorsing the kind of healthy breakfast food that helps cowboys stay on horseback longer.

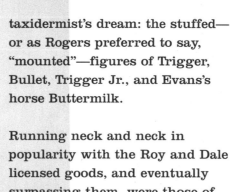

taxidermist's dream: the stuffed—or as Rogers preferred to say, "mounted"—figures of Trigger, Bullet, Trigger Jr., and Evans's horse Buttermilk.

Running neck and neck in popularity with the Roy and Dale licensed goods, and eventually surpassing them, were those of Hopalong Cassidy. William Boyd owned the rights to his sixty-six Hopalong Cassidy films from the 1930s and 1940s. When he syndicated them on television in the 1950s Hoppy became more popular than ever, winning legions of young fans, and Hopalong Cassidy merchandise took the country by storm. Boyd first signed an endorsement deal in April 1949, resulting in his becoming "the cowboy hero world's mightiest merchandiser," according to cowboy collectible authority Ted Hake. By the early 1950s, an estimated 2,500 Hoppy products were available; in 1952 alone, $20 million worth of Hoppy items were sold.

When Hoppy was featured on the cover of the June 12, 1950, issue of *Life*, he was described as a "cowboy juggernaut [who] penetrates every dwelling which has young children…. American youth is more aware of Hoppy than earlier generations ever were of Buffalo Bill, Lindbergh,

Babe Ruth or other idols of the past…. American children can well afford these days to pay $36 each for his black Western hats. Together with black shirt and pants, kerchief and steerhead clasp (called a 'concho'), boots and silver spurs, this constitutes the standard public Hoppy uniform." One inside photo showed eight youngsters decked out in Hoppy merchandise. The caption read: "Hoppy clothes from Lord & Taylor in New York, one of many stores with Hopalong Cassidy Hitching Posts, show a wide price range…leather jacket ($42.50); denim pants and shirt ($21.78); girls' frontier set ($27.80); paneled shirt set ($29.30); cheapest girls' Hoppy outfit ($4.95, with hat $1.95 extra); suit with leisure jacket ($42.75)." *Life* also reported that New York's Gimbel's Department Store had "placed an initial order for $22,500 worth of Hopalong Cassidy snow suits" and predicted that Boyd would rake in an estimated $800,000 from his share of the $70 million worth of merchandise sold in 1950. Among the licensed Hoppy products were cameras, clocks, bicycles, earmuffs, lunchboxes, and radios.

Just as Hoppy vouched for the benefits of consuming certain types of cereals, ice cream, tuna fish, instant pudding, milk, and bread, he included a message to kids with Hopalong Cassidy watches manufactured by the U.S. Time Corporation: "Hi Pardner! Time is the most important thing in your lives. Even one minute wasted is a moment lost that could have been spent in helping you to be a better and happier person.... Wrong as it is to waste your own time, it is even worse to waste the time of your friends. Be prompt and punctual in your appointments.... I sincerely hope that this watch will be a means of bringing you great joy, happiness, and success by keeping track of every minute of every hour of your most important TIME. Good luck. Hoppy."

The 1950s offered the widest variety of cowboy hero products, with buckaroos getting heavy airplay in film, radio, and television, as well as in books and comic books. "From licensed merchandise to premiums," according to Hake, "if a youngster could consume, play with, or somehow use a product, most likely something was available with a cowboy hero tie-in."

The trend of endorsed products by childhood heroes continued in the 1960s, but space rangers, soldiers, and secret agents began replacing buckaroos; as celebrity cowboys vanished from the screen and radio, they likewise diminished in popularity as kids' licensors. All those thousands of items from the 1930s, 1940s, and 1950s became coveted collectors' items. Not until *Toy Story,* with its cowboy doll hero Woody, did buckaroo-endorsed merchandise return for a new generation of kids. In fact, the plot of the delightful sequel, *Toy Story 2,* which added the characters of Jessie the Cowgirl and Bullseye the Horse, focuses on the popularity of Woody products in the 1950s and their subsequent value as collectors' items.

135

"Hi Pardner! Time is the most important thing in your lives. Even one minute wasted is a moment lost that could have been spent in helping you to be a better and happier person."

The ultimate Lone Cowboy outfit is shown, opposite. This play costume is reversible; turn it inside out, swap the feathered headdress for a Stetson and, yee-hah, Crazy Horse becomes the Bronco Kid. The Hopalong watch, above, is presumably designed to keep track of High Noon.

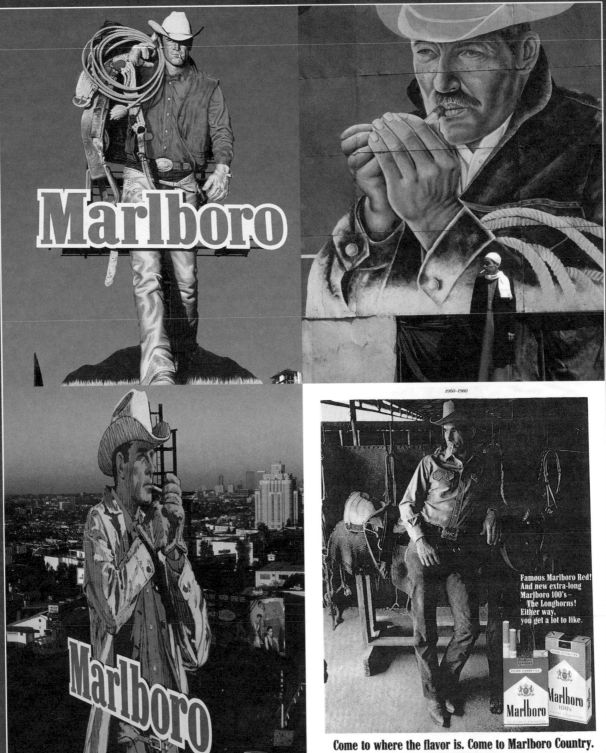

Famous Marlboro Red! And new extra-long Marlboro 100's— The Longhorns! Either way, you get a lot to like.

Come to where the flavor is. Come to Marlboro Country.

Children were not the only targets for products graced with cowboys. Once again, ordinary household goods emblazoned with buckaroos became huge with adults as they embraced the new Westerns on television in the 1950s and 1960s. Wildly popular programs such as *Bonanza* and *Gunsmoke* got their own merchandise, while generic cowpunchers could be found on all kinds of home furnishings, knickknacks, fabric and wallpaper, and decorative functional items like glasses, crockery, and—especially—ashtrays.

The cowboy's image in advertising products— ranging from automobiles, tobacco, and whiskey, to soda pop, clothing lines like Wrangler, Levi's, and Ralph Lauren, and perfume like Chaps—has remained prevalent. Marlboro cigarettes, in particular, have been strongly associated with range riders ever since the Marlboro Man advertising campaign was first conceived in 1954. Though he was banned from television in the 1970s for promoting bad habits, he still rides the range on billboards and magazine pages. Twelve years after the rough 'n' tumble cowboy's appointment as sole spokesman for the brand in 1964, Marlboros became the best-selling cigarette in the world. Improved filter tips helped, but perhaps the power of the cowboy image is what most influenced smokers—the reckless Tom Mix–style daredevils of today—to take up the brand buckaroos seemingly endorse.

The many moods of Marlboro Man (opposite) as he lopes through his mythical country were captured in a powerful marketing campaign that used the iconic outdoor image to sell a product to people who spent their days, not in the saddle but corralled in the high-rise gulches of urban America. Cowgirls are shown above on the catwalk in 1978, when the king of outdoor chic, Ralph Lauren, sent his pistol-packin' models moseyin' out in chaps, duster, wide-brim, and boots, tipping his hat to the resurgence of the Western genre. Beer endorsed by cowboys dusty from the trail (right) is sold by the barrel-load to office-bound city slickers.

138

A vengeful James Stewart (above) plays Jeff Webster in *The Far Country* (1954), directed by Anthony Mann, master of the noir Western. *The Sons of Katie Elder* (directed by Henry Hathaway, 1965,) marked the 58-year-old John Wayne's return to the screen after cancer surgery (opposite) and the first of his roles as the elder statesman of the purple sage.

The Shootists
Gary Cooper, John Wayne, Randolph Scott, and James Stewart

SOME OF AMERICA'S MOST DISTINCTIVE ACTORS CUT THEIR TEETH IN WESTERNS, IN THE PROCESS CREATING INDELIBLE IMAGES OF THE AMERICAN COWBOY. THE WORK OF GARY COOPER, JOHN WAYNE, RANDOLPH SCOTT, AND JAMES STEWART DURING THE GOLDEN AGE OF THE WESTERN—THE 1940S AND 1950S—FURTHERED THE CONCEPT OF THE TRAILBLAZER'S RUGGED INDIVIDUALISM.

GARY COOPER

Gary Cooper's roots in the Western go all the way back to its earliest days. He acted in many different types of films, but every few years would return to the Western, giving some of the strongest performances of his career.

Gary Cooper actually spent much of his childhood in the West. Born Frank James Cooper in Helena, Montana, in 1901, he was the son of immigrants who had come to Montana from England. His father was a doctor who worked with local Native Americans. Young Frank was sent off to England to attend school but hated it there and came back to Montana, where he eventually went to college in Bozeman. He then studied art at Grinnell College in Iowa and became a newspaper cartoonist.

He eventually found his way back West, ending up in California and working on silent movies as an extra. Primarily doing stunt riding, he made nearly fifty silent Westerns—about one per week. In 1926, he finally got to play the lead in a Zane Grey story, *Arizona Bound*, along with his horse Flash.

It was with the coming of sound, though, that Cooper really developed as an actor. His slow, understated, soft-spoken delivery, simmering-just-beneath-the-surface intensity, and extraordinary good looks made him a natural to star in 1929's *The Virginian*, directed by Victor Fleming. Cooper's long, lean form, sheathed in fringed leather chaps, along with his quiet, introverted quality as the hero, struck a chord with audiences. Though the following year he appeared in *The Spoilers* and *Fighting Caravans*, he didn't act in another Western until 1936. In that year, his performance as Wild Bill Hickok in Cecil B. DeMille's *The Plainsman* was applauded by critics and audiences alike.

In 1940, Cooper played a hardscrabble cowhand in William Wyler's well-crafted *The Westerner*, opposite Walter Brennan as the scene-stealing Judge Roy Bean. Cooper, however, held his own, with his portrayal being cited by film historian William Everson as "one of his best roles."

But it was the role of marshal Will Kane in 1952 that immortalized Cooper. *High Noon* was written as an allegory for the Red Scare witch-hunt in Hollywood of purported Communist sympathizers. Colleagues turned against one another to protect themselves; those accused by Senator McCarthy or the House Un-American Activities Committee faced Hollywood blacklisting. Cooper's performance as the haggard yet dignified Kane, who is abandoned by everyone in town and must face alone four vengeful outlaws, perfectly complements his role as the Virginian, who follows a personal code of ethics no matter the cost.

Cooper's personal life also played a part in his bitter, agonizing performance. His health wasn't good, with a severe stomach ulcer causing him a great deal of pain during filming. Also, he had recently been embroiled in scandal due to his tumultuous love affair with Patricia Neal, his costar in *The Fountainhead*. Cooper's Catholic wife, Rocky, refused to grant him a divorce, resulting in tabloid fodder sensationalizing the situation and causing the private Cooper great embarrassment and despair. (Eventually, he and Neal broke up and Cooper returned to his wife.) Cooper won his second Academy Award for best leading man for *High Noon*, later saying of the role, "It demanded everything I had—and I gave it all I had."

Between 1948 and 1959, Cooper made ten Westerns. Among the highlights in the last decade of his life was his performance in Anthony Mann's brutal 1958 film *Man of the West*. Cooper's driven antihero Link Jones has to track down and kill his murderous stepbrother and stepfather before he can find peace. Cooper's final Western performance came the following year in another violent film: *The Hanging Tree*. He died of cancer in Los Angeles in May, 1961.

141

The tot Gary Cooper (opposite) demonstrates the effect of early imprinting. The white hat indicates that he will follow the hero trail. Forsaken by all, including his deputies (left), Marshal Will Kane walks alone to his destiny facing four outlaws (above) in Fred Zinnemann's masterful, ambiguous *High Noon* (1952), made at the height of the McCarthy witch-hunts when standing up and being counted was dangerous. John Wayne, Charlton Heston, Marlon Brando, and Gregory Peck reportedly all turned the part down.

JOHN WAYNE: FROM MESQUITEER TO THE RINGO KID

T he most iconic Western hero of all time, John Wayne came to be synonymous with the role he played: a determined man of honesty, loyalty, and integrity. Over the course of his long career, the boundaries gradually blurred between the man and his character in Westerns. Wayne perpetuated this notion, once saying, "All I can do is sell sincerity, and I've been selling the hell out of it."

Wayne was born Marion Morrison in Winterset, Iowa, in 1907; two years later his family moved to Southern California. He got his lifelong nickname "Duke" when local firemen started calling him by the name of his constant companion, a pet Airedale. After graduating from Glendale High in 1925, he landed a football scholarship to the University of Southern California. He was dropped from the team in 1927 and left school, finding work at Fox studios as a prop man and an extra—the myth was later circulated that he was hired by Tom Mix in exchange for

football tickets. At Fox he met director John Ford, who cast him in a bit part in 1929's *Salute*, in which he played a Naval Academy student.

Later that year Wayne got his first big break when Raoul Walsh offered him the lead in his epic Western drama, *The Big Trail*. Stories vary as to how Wayne got the role; some believe Ford recommended him to Walsh, who had wanted the unavailable Cooper for the part. Walsh said he'd noticed Wayne when he

was a Fox prop man, and liked the way he walked. For *The Big Trail*, "Duke" Morrison took top billing as John Wayne, thanks to Walsh and director Edmund Goulding, who gave him the name. Playing a young frontier scout, Wayne cut quite the dashing figure in his buckskin garb and flowing locks. His acting was still quite tentative, though, and as the Depression hit, the film tanked. With it went Wayne's opportunity to star in more big movies—at least for a decade. The commercial failure of *The Big Trail* also contributed to studios refraining from investing in big-budget Westerns throughout the 1930s.

Wayne spent the next ten years making a string of budget films for Columbia, Warner Bros., Monogram, and Republic—"each one lousier than the last," he later complained. Early on, he played secondary characters in pictures with Buck Jones and Tim McCoy. His films for Warner Bros. found him remaking Ken Maynard silents, with the original footage of Maynard's

143

John Wayne (opposite), the cowboy's cowboy. Wayne (above), in Raoul Walsh's *The Big Trail* (1930), has his first leading role. Overnight success did not follow.

amazing riding stunts being juxtaposed with Wayne scenes. Not much of a horseman himself (he reportedly hated riding), Wayne was coached by the stuntman/actor/second-unit director Yakima Canutt, who often stunted for Wayne. The two devised superlative techniques for staged fistfights, which became the industry standard.

One of Wayne's oddest roles was as Singin' Sandy Saunders for a short-lived Monogram series. Even before the singing cowboy craze, Wayne starred as the humming gunslinger, with a dubbed-in croon by a nameless vocalist. More typically, though, the big-hatted cowpoke played by Wayne went by the name John. In 1932's *Ride 'Em Cowboy*, his horse was called Duke. Wayne's best work was for Republic, where he came under contract in the mid-1930s. As well as starring in numerous B's, Wayne was cast to replace Bob Livingston in the Three Mesquiteer series.

During the 1930s, Wayne made as many as eight B-Westerns a year; by now, his trademark mannerisms—a swagger of a walk and a kind of halting, rather intimidating style of speaking— were already well developed. Though at the mercy of the studios as to the roles he played, he developed a style that he would cultivate throughout his career. As his model was more Harry Carey than Tom Mix, Wayne later explained, "I made up my mind that I was going to play a real man to the best of my ability. I felt many of the Western stars of the '20s and '30s were too goddamn perfect. They never drank or smoked. They never wanted to go to bed with a beautiful girl. They never had a fight.... They were too goddamn sweet and pure to be dirty fighters. Well, I wanted to be a dirty fighter if that was the only way to fight back.... I was trying to play a man who gets dirty, who sweats sometimes, who

enjoys really kissing a gal he likes, who gets angry, who fights clean whenever possible but will fight dirty if he has to. You could say I made the Western hero a roughneck."

John Ford gave Wayne the chance to become the actor he wanted to be and to achieve stardom while doing so. In 1939 he cast him as the Ringo Kid in his groundbreaking film *Stagecoach*. On location in Utah's stunning Monument Valley desert, Ford worked Wayne hard, admonishing him "to act with his eyes not his mouth." *Stagecoach* marked Monument Valley's debut as Ford's favorite Western film location. Wayne claimed he turned Ford on to the Utah location, which he said he discovered while serving as prop man for a George O'Brien picture; Ford took credit for the discovery himself. The film was a resounding success with critics and audiences, sparking the resurgence of well-funded A-Westerns during a time when the B's ruled. Over the next decade and more, Hollywood's biggest actors would vie to star in Westerns.

As the Ringo Kid, Wayne played a combination gunslinging killer and softhearted innocent with more nuance than he'd previously demonstrated. Smitten with Claire Trevor's soiled dove, Dallas, the Kid is transformed from revenge-seeking ex-con to lovelorn homesteader, after protecting the stagecoach from Indian attack with such daring heroics as climbing from the racing coach to horseback (an astonishing stunt performed by Canutt) and defeating a rival gang in Lordsburg. Ford's loving close-ups of Wayne's face established his iconic nature for years to come. Western film historian Jon Tuska pointed out that Wayne, as consummate Western hero, "learned his ambling walk from Yakima Canutt, his granite resolve from Buck Jones, and his belief in human relationships from John Ford."

144

Ten years after his first star vehicle, Wayne's big break, playing honorable roughneck the Ringo Kid, came in John Ford's *Stagecoach* (1939). Ford held out for Wayne to play the role, to the point of seeking independent financing after big studios refused to risk an unknown lead in the film.

True Grit

Though Wayne had to fulfill his contract with Republic—making four more Mesquiteer films, for a total of eight—he was on his way to bigger things. He starred in a total of fifteen movies directed by Ford, including some non-Westerns. In 1948 he played cattleman Tom Dunson in Howard Hawks's superb Chisholm Trail epic *Red River* (1948). Wayne initially resisted the offer of the role, hesitating to play an old man. Over the course of the film, he ages from young buck to grizzled autocrat, demonstrating increased range as an actor, particularly in the emotional confrontations with his adopted son Matthew Garth, played by the striking Montgomery Clift in his first ever screen lead. *Red River* made Wayne an even bigger star than before.

Wayne's characterization of aging cavalry officer Nathan Brittles in Ford's *She Wore a Yellow Ribbon* (this the 1949 installment of his cavalry trilogy) continued in this direction, with the tough but vulnerable Brittles wiping his eyes when presented with a retirement gift by his troops.

In the 1950s and early 1960s, Wayne peaked as a gruff veteran Westerner in such roles as Hondo Lane in *Hondo* (1953), based on a Louis L'Amour story; the relentless Ethan Edwards, who doggedly pursues his kidnapped niece Debbie in Ford's 1956 opus *The Searchers*; the courageous and resourceful sheriff in *Rio Bravo*, Howard Hawks's 1959 film response to *High Noon*; and grizzled Tom Doniphon, the protagonist of another Ford classic, *The Man Who Shot Liberty Valance* (1962), an exploration of the mythologizing of the Western hero. In *The Searchers*, Wayne growls the words "That'll be the day," providing inspiration for a young Texas moviegoer named Buddy Holly. *Rio Bravo* teamed Wayne with inimitable codger Walter Brennan, along with such unlikely costars as ingénue Angie Dickinson, who plays the sheriff's love interest, Feathers; Italian-American crooner Dean Martin as his alcoholic deputy; and teen idol Ricky Nelson as his guitar-strumming, gun-wielding protégé. A more classic pairing occurs in *Valance* with Wayne's crusty buckaroo Tom Doniphon teaching

Wayne, Dean Martin, and Ricky Nelson (above left) and Wayne and Walter Brennan (opposite), are the law in Hawks's *Rio Bravo* (1959), made because neither Hawks (nor Wayne) could stand *High Noon. True Grit* (1969) was the movie that introduced U.S. Marshal Reuben J. "Rooster" Cogburn (above right) and delivered Wayne's only-ever Oscar.

pacifist attorney/future Senator Ranse Stoddard (James Stewart) how to defend himself against the vicious killer Liberty Valance. Doniphon's demise, along with a broken-down old stagecoach that first transported a starry-eyed Stoddard to the frontier, symbolizes the end of the rough 'n' tumble West. They also illustrate how fact is transformed into myth.

As traditional Westerns vanished from the screen in the late 1960s and early 1970s, Wayne became the last of a breed. The older and more beat-up he got, the better an actor he became. In 1965, he lost a lung to cancer but returned soon after to moviemaking, starring in Henry Hathaway's *The Sons of Katie Elder*. Wayne's aging deputy in *True Grit* (1969) may be the best performance of his career. Playing against a young, "liberated" Kim Darby, Wayne's character has gone to seed but still sticks by his old Western ways, getting the job done in the process. Film historian William Everson points out

that Wayne "reveals a subtlety and an honest warmth...that has rarely been displayed before." Wayne won an Oscar for his performance.

In the last decade of his life, Wayne continued to play similar roles, culminating in *Rooster Cogburn*, his 1975 pairing with Katharine Hepburn. By then, he was being called to task for his conservative political views; for example, his 1973 film, *Cahill, U.S. Marshal*, made by his own production company, was picketed by Native American activists, whose signs and placards decried Wayne as "the worst Indian killer in history" for his body of work.

His elegiac finale *The Shootist* (1976) showed his life's work in a more positive, albeit bittersweet, light, with numerous flashbacks from Wayne's previous films depicting the dying gunfighter's life. Three years later John Wayne lost his long battle against cancer.

Like Wayne, Southern-born Randolph Scott acted in both A- and B-movies. His style combined the austerity of William Hart with the subtlety of Gary Cooper. Hailing from Virginia and North Carolina, Scott never lost his genteel drawl; one of his first jobs in Hollywood was coaching Gary Cooper on his accent for *The Virginian*. In the early 1930s, Scott was cast in a series of nine pictures based on Zane Grey stories. In 1936 he played his first major role, Hawkeye, in *The Last of the Mohicans*.

Scott's chiseled good looks and soft-spoken, rather passive, manner made him an unassuming kind of Westerner. After World War II, he focused almost entirely on Westerns, acting in forty-two of them—more than any other star.

Scott played both good guys and outlaws, but even when he was acting the bad guy, his characterizations radiated a basic decency. He was the only moral lawman (Marshal Will Wright) in Henry King's pro-outlaw *Jesse James* (1939), evincing a wounded quality when James is double-crossed by the authorities. However, his characters' moral integrity never precludes his choosing the saloon-girl floozy over the virginal shopkeeper, as in *Abilene Town* (1946), or bamboozling his old buddy, played by Joel McCrea, in Sam Peckinpah's masterful *Ride the High Country* (1962). The latter presaged a new type of Western like *The Shootist*, featuring aging stars in elegiac roles.

After the demise of the B's in 1954, Scott continued to shoot some two Westerns a year. These moderate-budget pictures had some of the action qualities of the oaters, but A-grade production values. Forming a production company with veteran producer Harry Joe Brown, Scott made a series of compelling collaborations with director Bud Boetticher. Among

Randolph Scott with Nancy Gates (left) star in Bud Boetticher's *Comanche Station* (1960), one of the greatest roles of Scott's forty-two Westerns. Not all heroes come from the West; one of Scott's first major roles (opposite) was the trapper and woodsman Hawkeye in George B. Seisz's *Last of the Mohicans*, set during the French–Indian wars in colonial America.

SCOTT AND STEWART

the highlights were *The Tall T* (1957), *Buchanan Rides Alone* (1958), and in 1960 *Comanche Station*; in all of them, Scott usually played a driven loner. "The Boetticher hero as created by Scott can be said to possess or be moving toward a great serenity," says British film scholar Jim Kitses, "with the knowledge that we are fundamentally alone, that nothing lasts, that what matters in the face of all this is 'living the way a man should.'" He is a "man who endures through intelligent calculation and an overriding capacity for self-control in the face of

adversity." In his last picture, *Ride the High Country*, Scott brought these attributes to his lawman-turned-shyster showman who betrays the McCrea character to make one last score, then relents and finds redemption, surviving a shoot-out. After retiring, Scott lived another twenty-five years, dying in 1987.

James Stewart, by no means known only for his Western films, is best remembered for his role in Frank Capra's *It's a Wonderful Life*. He brought to

Stewart was just one of the cowboy megastars embroiled in *How the West Was Won* (1962), a sprawling epic that needed three high-octane directors (Henry Hathaway, John Ford, and George Marshall) to break it in, but is chiefly remembered as the first and only Western filmed in Cinerama. Marlene Dietrich (opposite) as Frenchy bringing a little Berlin *Schadenfreude* to the boys in the backroom in *Destry Rides Again* (1939).

his cowboys a vulnerable quality toughened by a stubborn willfulness. The Pennsylvania-born actor's distinctive voice and phrasing also added to his characters' sense of humanity. Stewart's first major Western role was the lead in the 1939 version of *Destry Rides Again*, opposite Marlene Dietrich as the conniving saloon singer Frenchy. With his signature bumbling quality, Stewart seemed much more apt as the antistud Tom Destry described in Max Brand's novel than Tom Mix, who was the star of the 1932 version. Ordering a glass of milk in the raucous Last Chance saloon, Destry symbolizes the complete opposite of the standard-issue macho lawman. He uses his wits rather than his guns to resolve most situations, including "taming" the man-eater Frenchy, though he turns out to be as good a shot as his renowned gunslinging father.

From the 1950s, Stewart focused almost entirely on Westerns, and gave some of his best work. Apart from his outstanding performance in *The Man Who Shot Liberty Valance*, he teamed with Wayne (and a slew of others) in the overblown Cinerama epic *How the West Was Won* (1962). He also acted in Wayne's final film, *The Shootist*, and in Ford's Western farewell,

Cheyenne Autumn (1964). *Broken Arrow* (1950), in which Stewart plays Tom Jeffords, was one of Hollywood's first attempts to positively portray Native Americans in a sympathetic light. Seeking peace with tribal leader Cochise (Jeff Chandler), Tom learns to speak Apache, then falls in love with and marries Indian maiden Sonseerey (Debra Paget). Sonseerey is then murdered by whites, a devastating scene that elicits one of Stewart's most emotionally raw performances.

Western auteur Anthony Mann greatly respected Stewart's work, and they collaborated on a number of films. Their first effort together, *Winchester '73* (1950), finds Stewart as Linn McAdam on a relentless search for the man who murdered his father. In this revenge classic, Stewart interrupts his quest to aid blond floozy Shelley Winters and an inexperienced Cavalry unit from attack by Indians. Stewart's multidimensional character study is at its best when it is disclosed that the killer McAdam seeks is his

own brother. As Kitses describes him, McAdam is "the model of stability and decorum in all respects except where his own brother is concerned, the mere sign of whom dements the character."

In *The Man from Laramie* (1955), as Will Lockhart, Stewart is again fixated on revenge—this time to find the persons responsible for supplying guns to the Indians, who used them to kill his brother's cavalry unit. Brutally dragged through fire and shot in the hand at close range, Stewart is not afraid to nearly fall apart or break down in tears. His vulnerability, combined with his ultimate tenacity, make for a very

likable hero. Stewart also starred in Mann's *Bend of the River*, *Naked Spur* (both 1952), and *The Far Country* (1954).

Through their very different characterizations of Western heroes, Cooper, Wayne, Scott, and Stewart created a multitextured portrait of the cowboy archetype. Their colleagues Joel McCrea, Henry Fonda, Gregory Peck, and Glenn Ford also made important contributions to this portrait. They turned out to be the last generation of actors to give so much of their screen time to the cowboy. Only a few lone guns would emerge to step into their boots.

James Stewart (opposite, top) cameos as Wyatt Earp in Ford's 1964 *Cheyenne Autumn*, the director's attempt to make up for his earlier, harsher portrayals of Indian nations. Up against the odds as the flawed avenger in *The Man from Laramie* (1955), Stewart (opposite, bottom) suffers but is undeterred. The character he created, Will Lockhart, was strong enough to spawn a TV series. Stewart suffers the conseq es of murderous racism (above) in Delmer Daves's *Broken Arrow* (1950).

154

Barbara Stanwyck, the definitive screen Annie Oakley, in George Stevens's 1935 imaginative biopic. The apple-pie queen herself, Doris Day (above right), scruffed up a treat to play Calam' as an irresistible singing tomboy in David Butler's *Calamity Jane* (1953).

Queens of the West
REEL (AND REAL) COWGIRLS

IT'S A MAN'S WORLD, THE OLD SAYING GOES, AND NOWHERE IS THIS MORE TRUE THAN IN WESTERNS. THOUGH WOMEN WERE THERE DURING THE TAMING OF THE WEST, MOST OF THEM OPERATED BEHIND THE SCENES IN CONSTRICTED ROLES OF HOMESTEADER'S WIFE OR DAUGHTER.

Some, however, did master the skills of riding, roping, and shooting—a few becoming famous in the process. And it is these headstrong cowgirls who have fascinated filmmakers and audiences alike, while providing role models for future generations of independent women.

It's unclear when the term "cowgirl" was first applied to female range riders, but it entered the popular lexicon in 1899 thanks to Will Rogers and Teddy Roosevelt. Both men were knocked off their feet that year when they made the acquaintance of Lucille Mulhall, thirteen-year-old daughter of rancher Zack Mulhall. On the Mulhalls' Oklahoma spread, Lucille took to riding and roping just like her male counterparts. She surpassed the men at lassoing loose calves, roping the escaping bovines by their hind legs—no mean feat. She had started riding at age two. By eleven she had mastered the art of roping, with her quarry eventually including steers, jackrabbits, and even wolves. Treated to

started bagging small game—even though the kick from the shotgun broke her nose the first time she fired it. By the time she was twenty, she could best anybody at competition shooting, including roustabout marksman Frank Butler. After beating Butler at a local contest, she joined him on the road. The two married and traveled as a team, with Annie eventually taking over as shootist with Butler as her assistant. Naturally, the charismatic Oakley came to Buffalo Bill's attention; at the time, she was working a show with Sitting Bull, who treated her as a daughter. After she joined Cody's outfit in 1885, he reportedly told his troupe, "She's to be the only white woman with our show, and I want you boys to welcome her and protect her." She proved so popular with her amazing shooting and riding, however, that soon Bill added "a bevy of Beautiful Rancheras, genuine and famous frontier girls" to the tour. They included equestrienne Emma Lake Hickok, Wild Bill Hickok's stepdaughter, and Georgia Duffy, billed as "The Rough Rider From Wyoming."

Other Wild West shows did the same. Pawnee Bill promoted his sharpshooting wife, May, as headliner; according to his posters, the show also featured "beauteous, dashing, daring, and laughing Western girls." The 1912 program for the Miller Bros. 101 Ranch boasted about the troupe's "Wild West Girls Whose Throne is the Saddle...an element new to this community." The program went on to set the record straight, defining cowgirls as "a development of the stock-raising West comparing with the bachelor girl and the independent woman of the East. She is not of the new woman class—not of the sort that discards her feminine attributes and tries to ape the man, simply a lively, athletic young woman with a superfluity of nerve and animal spirits, with a realization that in affairs where skill is the chief qualification she has an equal chance with her brothers."

demonstrations of Lucille's horseback prowess, guests like Roosevelt and Rogers went back East raving about her accomplishments. So when Papa Mulhall decided to wrangle his kids and create his own family Wild West troupe, they had a ready-made audience. Lucille won star billing, even when Tom Mix and Rogers himself joined the show for a while. During a 1904 tour that included a stint at the St. Louis World's Fair, Lucille broke steer-wrestling records by roping, dropping, and tying three steers in just over two minutes. The Mulhall outfit hit New York the following year, winning Lucille more legions of fans—and such monikers as "Lassoer in Lingerie" and "Champion Lady Steer Roper of the World."

Lucille Mulhall actually had several cowgirl predecessors who likewise became well-known to audiences, the most famous, of course, being Annie Oakley. Born Phoebe Ann Moses in rural Ohio in 1860, she originally honed her sharpshooting skills to help put food on the table for her struggling, fatherless family. She was only eight when she

Little Sure Shot herself, Annie Oakley (above), drawn from life, and (opposite) in her publicity stills, brought the piston packin' thrills of the West to the cream of European society—once (at his request) she shot the ashes off the cigar in Kaiser Wilhelm II's mouth.

157

Saddle Gals

Women had long been developing skills as cowhands working on their fathers' or husbands' ranches. A few accompanied the menfolk on cattle drives and an even smaller number disguised themselves as men so they could really live the life of a buckaroo. The most famous of these was Jo Monaghan, who fled the East in 1870 after becoming a single mother, leaving her sister to raise her child. She threw on a pair of pants, a vest, and a hat, and passed herself off as a man, eventually running a small ranch in Idaho. Not until her death in 1904 was she discovered to be a woman (and in the 1990s a film, *The Ballad of Little Jo*, was based on her life).

Another famous cattlewoman was Lizzie Williams, who operated a huge Texas ranch in the late 1800s; she required her husband to sign an agreement stating that she was sole owner of the property. To further protect her interests, she joined her drovers up the Chisholm Trail to oversee the livestock transactions at the Kansas railhead. Between 1875 and 1900, nearly 250,000 women ran ranches or farms of their own.

The further West the ranches moved, however, the tougher it could be for a woman to gain acceptance as a cowhand unless she had the blessing of her husband or father. Ellen Watson, of Sweetwater Valley, Wyoming, was nicknamed Cattle Kate for her punching—some said rustling—acumen. She was lynched in 1889 by neighboring cattle barons who were greedy for her land. *The Cheyenne Daily Leader* summed up popular opinion of such a woman living outside society's norms, calling Watson a rustler and whore, and describing her thus: "Of robust physique, she was a daredevil in the saddle, handy with a six-shooter and adept with the lariat and branding iron. She rode straddle [rather than sidesaddle, which was then deemed proper for ladies], always had a vicious broncho for a mount and seemed never to tire of dashing across the range."

The *Daily Leader*'s language sounds exactly as if it belongs in a dime novel, and a few women did indeed begin to star in the pages of pulps. Though not exactly cowgirls, the two most notorious women of the West were Belle Starr and Calamity Jane. Starr died before the name "cowgirl" was even coined, but the descriptions of her in dime novels as an accomplished equestrienne

Calamity Jane took pen in hand herself to embroider her life story. Brought into the world as Martha Jane Cannary in 1852, she moved to Montana with her family as a girl and took up riding and shooting. Early on, she gave up petticoats and dresses for buckskin trousers and boots, seeking adventure on the range. She also never let the truth get in the way of a good story. Though she claimed to have served as a scout for Custer and to have secretly married Wild Bill Hickok, the facts don't bear her out. Having once ridden a bull through the streets of Rapid City, she made a name for herself as a hard-drinking, gunslinging rabble-rouser. Not just the heroine of the exaggerated memoir that she peddled at her Wild West show appearances, Calamity Jane was also the subject of a number of pulp novels. She succumbed to the side effects of her hard-living ways in Deadwood, South Dakota, in 1903.

and shootist helped define the term. She was born Myra Belle Shirley in 1846, the daughter of a prominent Missouri businessman. She shucked the straight life, throwing in her lot with a succession of outlaw lovers, who included Cole Younger, Jim Reed, Sam Starr, and Blue Duck. She bore their children and then joined in their robberies until an unknown assailant shot her in the back in 1889. That same year, her embellished "biography" was published; its cover showed her donning a cowboy hat and fringe with six-shooter in hand. The cover lines called her "The Bandit Queen, or the Female Jesse James."

The real Calamity Jane (top), was a rather more intimidating character than her celluloid imitators. Ken Kercheval plays Buffalo Bill, Jane Alexander Calamity, and Frederic Forrest Wild Bill Hickok in a sanitized version of the story made for TV in 1985.

Rodeo Belles

Calamity's bull riding may have been an inspiration to other Western gals, who practically grew up on horseback with a lasso in their hands. Just as they learned to master trick riding, steer roping, and broncobusting, these ranch-bred daughters had to conquer prejudice against their participation in the earliest organized rodeos offering prizes to contestants. Setting the standard as the daddy of 'em all, Cheyenne's Frontier Days began in 1897 and initially excluded women from its ranks. Women who had already gained fame through Wild West shows, circuses, and informal local competitions began lobbying for their inclusion, so "ladies' bronc riding" was added to the program in 1906. Through the efforts of early stars Bertha Blancett, Florence LaDue, and Lucille Mulhall, women were welcomed to participate from the beginning in the Pendleton Roundup and Calgary Stampede, major rodeos founded in 1911 and 1912 respectively. Fanny Sperry Steele, "Lady Bucking Horse Champ of the World" for 1912 and 1913, perhaps best described the cowgirl spirit in a 1976 reminiscence: "How can I explain to dainty, delicate women what it is like to climb down into a rodeo chute onto the back of a wild horse? How can I tell them it is a challenge that lies deep in the bones.... Perhaps it is odd that a woman should be born with an all-consuming love of horseflesh.... It seems to me as normal as breathing air or drinking water, that the biggest thing on my horizon has been the four-legged critter with mane and tail."

These daredevil women who braved bucking horses and ferocious steers became huge favorites with audiences. Beginning in the 1920s, they popularized trousers and short bobbed hair, as did their flapper sisters back East. Flamboyant dressers such as trick rider Fox Hastings helped to create the flashy Western style taken to the movies by Tom Mix. However, after a tragic accident at the 1929 Pendleton Roundup in which bronc rider Bonnie McCarroll was killed during the bucking horse competition, rodeos began eliminating the "dangerous" categories for women contestants, until only barrel racing and fancy riding remained.

160

Helen Gibson (opposite) was first wife of cowboy Hoot, and took over the first aid box from Helen Holmes in the title role of the *Hazards of Helen* (1915). She specialized in Western stunts and played Calamity Jane in the movie *Custer's Last Stand* (1936).

CELLULOID COWGIRLS

162

Some female trick riders found work in early motion pictures. Del Jones, a star attraction with the Miller Bros. 101 Ranch, got stunt work in Westerns, even doubling for Douglas Fairbanks in such films as *The Knickerbocker Buckaroo* (1919). In the earliest days of filmmaking, though, cowgirls were something of a rarity on-screen. Annie Oakley starred in an Edison Kinescope, and the character of Calamity Jane was the topic of five silent films. But most of the gals were damsels in distress, rescued by heroes such as Broncho Billy or Bill Hart, or tied to a railroad track, as in the *Perils of Pauline* serial. There were a few early exceptions. *Western Girls*, in 1911, told the tale of a pair of sisters who disguised themselves as cowboys to capture a gang of bad guys. A couple of serials, *The Girl From Frisco* and *The American Girl*, starred real-life ranch gal Marin Sais as a crime-solving cowgirl. D. W. Griffith regular Dorothy Gish played a desperada in fringed chaps, black Montana Peak, and gunbelt in 1919's *Nugget Nell*, a fictional outlaw in turn-of-the-century dime novels, inspired by Belle Starr. And in the 1920s, Tom Mix's daughter Ruth acted in a handful

of Westerns, getting work as "a chip off the old block"— supposedly to her father's dismay.

The first actor to take on the cowgirl role in a series of pictures was feisty "Texas" Guinan. Born Mary Louise Cecilia Guinan in Waco, Texas, in 1884, she started her career as a chorus girl in Times Square music halls. To make a name for herself, she donned black lace chaps and trotted down a ramp on horseback through a New York City theater, twirling her lasso. Sure enough, "after the show a movie man signed me up [for] a two-reel Western," she later recalled. As a no-nonsense, pants-wearing cowgirl wielding a whip and revolver, Guinan starred in such films as 1917's *Get Away Kate*, 1918's *Two Gun Woman*, and 1921's *The Girl Sheriff*.

Once sound came to Westerns, only the occasional buckarette made an appearance. In 1936, the lovely blonde Jean Arthur played a vivacious Calamity Jane in Cecil B. DeMille's *The Plainsman*. The fireworks between her Jane and Gary Cooper's Hickok helped create the false notion that the two were an item. (Most Western historians think Calamity and Hickok never actually met,

Jane Frazee (above) sat pretty on her horse through many pleasant musical Westerns, costarring with singing cowboys such as Roy Rogers. Jean Arthur (opposite) makes a convincing Calamity Jane in Cecil B. DeMille's *The Plainsman* (1936), in which Gary Cooper played her Wild Bill.

though Calamity Jane was clearly obsessed with him.) Two decades later, another perky blonde, Doris Day, took on the title role in *Calamity Jane*, in which she scored the hit "Secret Love."

Paving the way for singing cowgirls, Patsy Montana scored a 1934 million-selling record with the self-penned "I Want to Be a Cowboy's Sweetheart." Born Rubye Blevins in 1912 in Arkansas, Patsy popularized the cowgirl image as "the Yodeling Cowgirl from San Antone," followed by a stint with the Montana Cowgirls. She then joined the WLS Barn Dance in Chicago alongside singing cowboy Gene Autry. Montana only made one film appearance, in Autry's *Colorado Sunset* (1939), but continued to perform in her trademark cowgirl outfit until her death in 1998. Other popular singing cowgirls hitting Chicago's airwaves included the Girls of the Golden West and Louise Massey and the Westerners.

Hollywood's first singing cowgirl was Dorothy Page, who had started her career on the radio. She was cast in the role of ranch gal Shirley Martin, who kicked outlaws' butts in a string of late 1930s B-Westerns, including *Singing Cowgirl*, *Ride 'Em Cowgirl*, and *Water Rustlers*. Other B-Westerns starring Gene Autry and fellow cowboys also featured saddle gals, played by such actresses as June Storey, Evelyn Finley, Nell O'Day, Betty Miles, Iris Meredith, Jane Frazee, Penny Edwards, and Lois January. Some of them were superb riders; others were decidedly not, including Myrna Dell, who later remembered, "On the first day of the picture, I was supposed to get on a horse. I went over to Bob Livingston and whispered, 'Which side of the horse am I supposed to get up on?'... In those days, you'd get a lead in a B-Western and that would be your training."

Woman with a Whip

In the 1930s, Annie Oakley provided a major role for Barbara Stanwyck, an actress who eventually personified the tough-as-nails female range rider. This celluloid cowgirl actually grew up on the mean streets of Brooklyn, where she was born Ruby Stevens in 1907. Orphaned at four and relegated to foster homes, she started as an entertainer by dancing in the streets to the sounds of the hurdy-gurdy. This led to her getting work as a chorus girl, eventually hoofing it in the Ziegfeld Follies and in a musical revue organized by none other than Texas Guinan. After acting in a Broadway play, she landed a role in a silent film, which persuaded her to relocate to Hollywood in 1928. Seven years later, Stanwyck was cast in her first Western, 1935's *Annie Oakley*. Directed by George Stevens, the film took some license with the Oakley story, having her throw her first shooting match with Butler because she "couldn't beat that fellow—he was just too pretty." Overall, however, it was a fairly accurate portrayal, and Stanwyck became smitten with Westerns.

Her next was Cecil B. DeMille's 1939 epic *Union Pacific*, a saga covering the building of the first transcontinental railroad. Playing the spunky daughter of a train engineer, Stanwyck performed all her own stunts, a feat she repeated throughout her career. Costar Joel McCrea enthused that Stanwyck was "fearless and has more guts than most men." Her next Western role, in 1942's *The Great Man's Lady*, had her sliding down banisters, eloping on horseback, and shooting and dressing rabbits. Stanwyck relished action roles, and in 1950's *The Furies*, to director Anthony Mann's

Barbara Stanwyck (left) starts her Hollywood film career in *Annie Oakley*. "Whadda we do now, Barbara?" Ronald Reagan's character (shown opposite) is overwhelmed by Stanwyck, who is at the top of her range in *Cattle Queen of Montana* (Allan Dwan, 1954).

dismay, insisted on doing her own risky riding scenes rather than let a stunt double handle them. She once boasted, "I'm the best action actress in the world. I can do horse drags and jump off buildings, and I have the scars to prove it."

One of Stanwyck's most famous heroines was Sierra Nevada Jones, the headstrong cowgirl who drives herd from Texas to Montana with her father, only to be bushwhacked by Indians. *Cattle Queen of Montana* (1954) found her playing opposite future cowboy president Ronald Reagan, while earning the respect of her Blackfeet Indian colleagues by doing

all her own stunts. After the shoot, they awarded her with membership in their Brave Dog Society, citing her "very hard work—rare for a white woman," and giving her the honorary title "Princess Many Victories." In the film, the compact, red-haired Jones, clad in black Stetson, fringed vest, and skintight pants, befriends an Indian, shoots a lusty cowhand, and leaps astride her galloping stallion, scandalizing the town ladies— and bringing to mind ol' Cattle Kate. Fortunately, Sierra Jones prevails, beating out a villainous cattle baron who has ordered her father's death, stolen their land claim, and created conflict among the

Blackfeet by corrupting one faction with guns and liquor. Of course, Jones and the undercover cavalryman played by Reagan ride off together into the sunset— it was a B-movie, after all.

Stanwyck took on a total of ten Westerns in the 1940s and 1950s, including the roles of outlaw women in 1956's *The Maverick Queen*—the Sundance Kid's moll Kit Banion—and Samuel Fuller's violent 1957 Western, *Forty Guns*, originally entitled *Woman with a Whip*. Her best-known part came in the 1960s, though, as Virginia Barkley, iron-fisted matriarch of a San Joaquin ranch on television's *The Big Valley*, which ran from 1965 to 1969.

Stanwyck's strong-willed Western woman was taken up a notch by Joan Crawford's hard-bitten saloon-keeper Vienna, and Mercedes McCambridge's vicious ranchera Emma in Nicholas Ray's over-the-top *Johnny Guitar*. A favorite film of Martin Scorsese's, this 1954 Western psychodrama climaxes in a twisted shoot-out between the two female rivals, feuding over land rights and cowboy hide. It was Stanwyck's more tempered and realistic portrayals, however, that would stick with such actresses as Jane Fonda, Angelica Huston, and Jane Seymour, who would play the next generation of cowgirls.

Barbara Stanwyck (above) is tough cookie Kit Banion, the distaff side of the Wild Bunch, in *The Maverick Queen* (1956), directed by Western veteran Joseph Kane. Joan Crawford (opposite) wears the trousers in *Johnny Guitar* (1954) and brings her signature melodramatics to a characteristically button-lipped genre.

QUEEN OF THE WEST

In the 1940s, the lovely and talented Dale Evans took the ball from other singing cowgirls and ran with it. At Roy Rogers's side, she earned the title "Queen of the West," becoming the only woman ever to place in the Top 10 Most Popular Western Stars poll voted on by movie theater exhibitors. Ironically, the Texas-born singer/songwriter/actress grew up dreaming of being a Broadway chanteuse rather than a singing cowgirl. A few years after her birth in 1912, Frances Octavia Smith moved with her family from Uvalde, Texas, to rural Arkansas. When she was fourteen, she eloped with her first boyfriend, giving birth to their son the next year. After the marriage dissolved, she took her baby with her to Memphis, where she eventually found work singing on the radio.

With the new show-biz name of Dale Evans, given her by a Louisville program director, she struggled to achieve her career goals, singing in the South, Midwest, and Texas. In 1938, her jazz-tinged vocals won her spots on top Chicago-based radio programs and nightclubs, and her songwriting acumen resulted in the popular "Will You Marry Me, Mr. Larrimee." Hollywood beckoned. In 1941 she received a contract at Fox, but that yielded only bit parts. Two years later she signed with Republic, where she was given the lead in a country musical, *Swing Your Partner*. Eight pictures on, Dale's breakthrough came in 1944's *The Cowboy and the Senorita*. In it she played Ysobel Martinez, whose stolen family fortune is recovered by Roy Rogers.

Though she hit it off with her costar, Evans and her horse did not get along, as she later recalled: "I had not ridden since I was seven years old.

The fact was I couldn't ride worth beans. To make matters worse, they gave me a big horse with the disposition of a convict breaking out of prison—frisky to the point of being downright mean and with a mind of his own. How I stayed on my horse I'll never know. I bounced so hard in the saddle that my temporary caps just flew out of my mouth." Fortunately, Rogers encouraged his costar to get riding lessons, saying, "I never saw so much sky between a woman and a horse," and eventually Evans ended up with a more compatible steed named Pal (followed in television by Buttermilk).

After a string of successful pairings with Rogers, Evans resisted being "typecast as a Western character" and ventured out in a few other types of roles. She soon returned to Roy for good, admitting, "The chemistry was just right between [Roy and me], apparently, because after I made one picture with him, the exhibitors said, 'Don't break the team up.'" In her twenty-eight films with Rogers, Evans's character was always smart, independent, and outspoken. She played journalists, scientists, novelists, entertainers, and "dudeens" (the female equivalent of dudes) who by the film's end become bona fide cowgirls, comfortably astride Pal and wearing her trademark Stetson and split skirt with bolero vest. Popular as she was with fans, though, in the film credits she usually took fourth billing, after Rogers's "costar" Trigger, "the Smartest Horse in the Movies," and Rogers's sidekick Gabby Hayes, Smiley Burnette, Andy Devine, or Pat Brady.

Among her many achievements, Evans wrote the classic theme song "Happy Trails" for Roy. She and Roy were married in 1947 after he proposed while

169

Dale Evans, the Rhinestone Queen of the West and fitting consort to Roy Rogers, presented the polar opposite of the hard-bitten cattle queens and saloon owners of the 1950s films.

"I never saw so much sky between a woman and a horse."

the two were appearing at a rodeo. Dale and Roy moved into television in 1951, creating *The Roy Rogers Show*, in which Evans runs a café in Mineral City but spends much of her time chasing crooks with Roy. Her film and TV character yielded a panoply of licensed merchandise for junior cowgirls, including outfits, play sets, books, comics, and more. Recording frequently with Rogers, Evans wrote another classic, "The Bible Tells Me So," and the pair continued to make personal appearances into their eighties. Even after she suffered a heart attack and stroke and being confined to a wheelchair, Dale Evans still dressed in bright fringed and appliqued cowgirl outfits to conduct interviews. She died in February 2001, a true cowgirl through and through—and an inspiration to millions.

Another television range rider who got her start in musical Westerns was Gail Davis, an Arkansas native who went to college in Texas. Unlike Evans, though, Davis was an amazing equestrienne and a crack shot. She began her career in Gene Autry films, eventually acting in fourteen—more than any of his other female costars. She

also performed in Autry's touring company, astounding audiences with her trick riding. She could stand up while galloping at breakneck speed around the arena or dangle precariously off the saddle, among other feats originated

by her predecessors in Wild West shows and rodeos. When Autry started his Flying A Productions to venture into television in the early 1950s, Davis was cast as the lead in *Annie Oakley*—the first woman to star in a Western series. This fantasized depiction of Oakley found her living with her kid brother Tag near the dusty desert town of Diablo. Wearing

a fringed cowgirl outfit decorated with bull's-eye targets and accented with fringe, the pigtailed sure-shot wrangled unscrupulous tinhorns and deadly train robbers, proving that women *could* get the job done—though she had to prove it most weeks to her skeptical deputy pal Lofty. The show continued for four years (1953–1957), spawning an Annie Oakley craze for young girls who could purchase such licensed goods as her cowgirl outfits, books, games, paper dolls, and puzzles, among numerous other items.

Davis, along with Evans and Stanwyck, certainly made an impact on ambitious young women of the future. One of the modern women they inspired to saddle a horse or make it in show biz was rodeo rider-cum-country singer Reba McEntire. McEntire eventually starred as Annie Oakley in a revival of the smash Broadway musical *Annie Get Your Gun*. Texas' Dixie Chicks—the biggest-selling female country trio of all time—put their gratitude in a song, "Thank Heavens for Dale Evans": "You're everything I ever want to be...Dale Evans made a cowgirl out of me."

170

Gail Davis (above) got her guns to play Annie Oakley in the first TV Western series with a female lead (1954). The series was the brainchild of Gene Autry, with whom Davis made 14 films between 1950 and 1953.
Dale Evans (right) leads her man's horse to water.

Ford lines up his Indians (below) for an attack on the eponymous stagecoach (opposite) in his signature movie of 1939. The staggering setting of Monument Valley, Utah—here seen for the first time in a Ford movie—was allegedly discovered by John Wayne, although Ford claimed the find as his own.

DIRECTORS JOHN FORD, HENRY KING, HOWARD HAWKS, AND ANTHONY MANN

NO ONE CONTRIBUTED AS MUCH TO THE WESTERN AS DIRECTOR JOHN FORD. HE STARTED HIS CAREER AS WESTERNS BEGAN AND RETIRED JUST AS THE GENRE WAS EMBARKING ON A RADICAL NEW DIRECTION. AS ITS POETIC MYTHMAKER, HE HAS BEEN CALLED THE GREAT ROMANTICIST OF THE WEST.

The cinematic visions of other directors who began work during the first half of the twentieth century have also enriched our idea of the West. Among the most prolific were Henry King, Howard Hawks, and Anthony Mann.

John Ford

From his earliest days in Hollywood, John Ford introduced himself by saying, "I'm John Ford, I make Westerns." But he did not make a Western with sound until 1939 with *Stagecoach*—his first since *Three Bad Men*, his 1926 follow-up to *The Iron Horse*. He had spent the 1930s exploring more personal themes, as in the Ireland-based drama *The Informer*, as well as directing pictures assigned to him by the studio. When Ford became smitten with the story for *Stagecoach* (Ernest Haycox's novel *Stage to Lordsburg*), he had to struggle to find

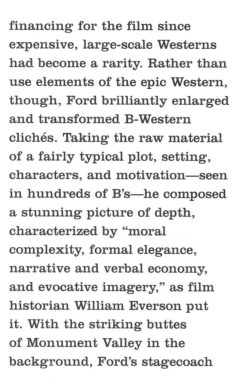

financing for the film since expensive, large-scale Westerns had become a rarity. Rather than use elements of the epic Western, though, Ford brilliantly enlarged and transformed B-Western clichés. Taking the raw material of a fairly typical plot, setting, characters, and motivation—seen in hundreds of B's—he composed a stunning picture of depth, characterized by "moral complexity, formal elegance, narrative and verbal economy, and evocative imagery," as film historian William Everson put it. With the striking buttes of Monument Valley in the background, Ford's stagecoach

makes a precipitous run between two towns. Along the way, the passengers are either killed or transformed by the journey. Ford elicited stellar performances from his cast, a combination of character actors such as Andy Devine and John Carradine, B-movie stalwart John Wayne, and top talent like Claire Trevor

and Thomas Mitchell, who won the best supporting actor Oscar for his role as the drunken Doc Boone. For the most part, those who stick together and help one another, forming a community, survive—but in the end Wayne and Trevor must leave town to start a new life. Ford's film revitalized the Western, in addition to giving Wayne's career its boost.

A passionate patriot, Ford spent the World War II years directing films for the government. His first postwar film was Henry Fonda's return to Westerns. Fonda had starred as Frank

John Wayne leaps into action as the Ringo Kid, the role that put him on the Western map (top). The film poster for *Stagecoach* (above) emphasizes Ford's theme of the pettiness of humanity in the face of nature's grandeur. A study in restless repose, Henry Fonda plays Wyatt Earp (opposite) in *My Darling Clementine* (1946), John Ford's take on the endlessly fascinating O.K. Corral incident.

James in both Henry King's 1939 film *Jesse James* and the following year's Fritz Lang–directed sequel, *The Return of Frank James*. Fonda and Ford collaborated, too, in the masterful *Grapes of Wrath* in 1940, and in 1943 Fonda had given an excellent performance in William Wellman's intensely dark psychological Western, *The Ox-Bow Incident*. As nuanced and rich as those roles were, Fonda surpassed them in the superb *My Darling Clementine*, as the conflicted marshal of Tombstone, Wyatt Earp. In its 1946 review, the *New York Times* said: "Fonda...shows us an elemental character who is as real as the dirt he walks on." The *Times* praised the film's "tone of pictorial authority.... Every scene, every shot is the product of a keen and sensitive eye— an eye which has deep comprehension of the beauty of rugged people and a rugged world." *Time* also raved about the film: "[Ford's] camera sometimes pauses, with a fresh childlike curiosity, to examine the shape and texture of a face, a pair of square-dancing feet, a scrap of desert landscape, or single dusty road. The leisurely lens...makes some of Ford's black and white sequences as richly lifelike as anything ever trapped in Technicolor."

"When the legend becomes a fact, print the legend."

Clementine climaxes with the infamous shoot-out at the O.K. Corral. Ford said his version had been inspired by reminiscences Earp shared while the two men caroused in the early 1900s. Ford claimed Earp had called it a carefully planned military attack, rather than a spontaneous gun battle. The film takes license with the tubercular Doc Holliday, however, played by the rather burly Victor Mature; Ford's Doc is an alcoholic surgeon rather than a dentist. Ford built his version of Tombstone near Monument Valley, straddling Arizona and Utah.

Monument Valley was also the setting for Ford's cavalry trilogy, *Fort Apache* (1948), *She Wore a Yellow Ribbon* (1949), and *Rio Grande* (1950), starring the director's "family" of actors—John Wayne, Ward Bond, Henry Fonda, Harry Carey Jr., and Ben Johnson, as well as veterans Shirley Temple, Mae Marsh (who started with D. W. Griffith), and former singing cowboy Dick Foran.

The characters' placement within the landscape was an important element of Ford's films, with the singularly shaped buttes of Monument Valley making for plenty of symbolism. Shot in color, *She Wore a Yellow Ribbon* won the Academy Award for best photography.

Also in color and partially filmed in Monument Valley, *The Searchers* (1956) is perhaps Ford's most stunningly visual picture. Though scenes shot right outside Los Angeles were juxtaposed with those in the magnificent Monument Valley, it worked somehow.

Sentimental and larger than life, Ford's Westerns also contributed to the mythologizing of the cowboy through their musical scores. Ford's films often featured music based on old cowboy ballads and American folk songs, keeping them alive in the national consciousness.

Big sky and small but indomitable riders (above) is a quintessential Ford shot from *The Searchers* (1956). James Stewart as The Man Who Shot Liberty Valance, John Wayne as The Man Who Actually Shot Liberty Valance, and Lee Marvin as The Man Who Is Liberty Valance (opposite), in the eponymous film of 1962.

In 1962, Ford held a magnifying glass up to the making of the cowboy myth in *The Man Who Shot Liberty Valance*. Over the course of the film, the oft-told fable behind Senator Ranse Stoddard's rise to political power is unraveled as a lie. When the truth is made known to the local newspaper, the reporter decides to stick with fiction over fact, cynically quipping, "When the legend becomes a fact, print the legend."

Of Ford's own work as a maker of legend, it has been said that he was on a "lifetime odyssey...to restore faith by probing into the past," but when asked about the motivations behind his films, the renowned curmudgeon usually shrugged off the question. He did once admit, however, "We've had a lot of people who were supposed to be great heroes and you know damn well they weren't. But it's good for the country to have heroes to look up to. Like Custer—a great hero! Well, he wasn't. Not that he was a stupid man, but he did a stupid job that day. On the other hand, of course, the legend always has some foundation."

In his later films, Ford seemingly addressed the domination of his mythmaking oeuvre by macho white men. *Sergeant Rutledge* (1960), starring African-American actor Woody Strode, told the story of a black cavalryman who was court-martialed on trumped-up charges. Ford's last Western, 1964's *Cheyenne Autumn*, starring James Stewart, was a sympathetic and compassionate depiction of a tortuous fifteen-hundred-mile trek made by three hundred Cheyenne to a reservation in 1878. It was almost thirty years before Kevin Costner's *Dances with Wolves*, though, and by the late 1960s violent Westerns featuring antiheroes had replaced Ford's more traditional heroic tales in the public's imagination. Ford retired from moviemaking, though he continued to visit John Wayne on location until he was sidelined by cancer. After Ford's death in 1973, Wayne said of his old associate, "He was an artist with a camera, a painter with a profound sense of color, shading, and light and shadow."

HENRY KING

irginia-born director Henry King enjoyed a career in movies as long as Ford's. He, too, started in the silent era, making such Westerns as *When a Man Rides Alone* (1918) and the comedy *Where the West Begins* (1919). Once sound came in, King undertook many different types of films but often returned to Westerns, specializing in large-scale historical dramas.

Jesse James, his 1939 romanticized look at one of America's most notorious outlaws, starred handsome matinee idol Tyrone Power as Jesse, alongside Henry Fonda's striking and sincere Frank James. The film focuses on the darkly combustible Jesse's struggle between the love of his fiancée, Zee, and his "moral" duty to right the wrong done his family by the powerful railroad company, forcing him into a life of crime. King and screenwriter Nunnally Johnson traveled to the James family's native Missouri to soak up atmosphere and interview people who had known Jesse or Frank, including Frank's son. King and Johnson took extraordinary liberty with the facts, however, to paint a pretty picture of the killers.

King's critically and commercially successful film started a trend toward glamorizing outlaws, presenting them as Robin Hood–style thieves forced by a corrupt society into criminal activity. With the country just recovering from the Great Depression, it's no surprise that audiences bought into the concept. A stream of outlaw films followed, including the film's 1940 sequel directed by Fritz Lang, *The Return of Frank James*; *When the Daltons Rode* (1940); *Bad Men of Missouri* (1941); *Billy the Kid* (1941); and *Belle Starr* (1941). "Over the next twenty years a Jesse James 'canon' developed in which themes, figures, scenes, and characters clearly derived from King's original treatment were continually varied, reprised, and reinterpreted," writes Richard Slotkin in *Gunfighter Nation*. "Many of these films borrowed images or cribbed actual footage from King's film, as if his images had become authenticating 'historical' references. The populist outlaw figure became an important symbol in the lexicon of movie mythology. Motifs, figures, and performers identified with the 'cult' could be used to give mythic/ideological resonance to other kinds of stor[ies]."

Interestingly, King later followed his glamorization of the outlaw with another important trend via his emotionally powerful Gregory Peck vehicle, 1950's *The Gunfighter*. This dark, moving film looks at what happens to the notorious outlaw who survives. Peck gives an incredibly empathic performance as Jimmy Ringo, a lonely man hounded by his own fame as one of the West's fastest guns. Everywhere he goes, young bucks challenge Ringo to draw, which he inevitably does to survive—ending up with another notch on his gun and another vengeful assassin on his trail. Like a cornered animal, Ringo cowers at a table in a saloon, where he's treated like a hero by a nostalgic bartender who then endangers Jimmy's life by spreading the word about his famous patron. Ringo's former running buddy is now the town marshal who must get the gun magnet out of town in one piece. The exhausted Ringo just wants to settle down on a little farm with his estranged wife—the town schoolmarm, natch!— and their son. But it's too late—his myth has grown to such proportions that he can't extricate himself from it. Ringo's chilling dying words to the young gun who finally shoots him in the back condemns his murderer to be haunted as he was, perpetuating the awful cycle. Perhaps it's no wonder that, decades later, Bob Dylan would claim *The Gunfighter* as an influence on his songwriting. The reclusive artist could probably relate to Ringo's haunted solitude as well.

Jesse James (opposite) is the legend according to Henry King, one of the many directors to use the story of the James brothers as the basis for their individual brand of Western mythologizing. Gregory Peck (right), handsome and doomed, as the fastest—and loneliest—gun in the West in *The Gunfighter* (1950), is King's study of the unbearable pressure of personal myth.

180

HOWARD HAWKS

L ike King, Howard Hawks made many types of films but occasionally directed large-scale historical Western dramas. Born in Indiana in 1896, he began his career as a prop boy at Paramount. He started directing in the 1930s, giving Walter Brennan his first important role in his 1935 film *Barbary Coast*. Hawks's most famous films, *Red River* and *Rio Bravo*, both starred John Wayne at his most testosterone-fueled. *Red River*, filmed on location in Arizona, fairly accurately depicts the realities of a grueling trail drive up the Chisholm Trail. Upon its release in 1948, some critics hailed the John Wayne–Montgomery Clift picture as the milestone Western of the decade. A cowboy version of *Mutiny on the Bounty* might aptly describe *Red River*. It revolves around rough 'n' tough Tom Dunson's increasingly tyrannical leadership being usurped

by his handsome, sharpshooting adopted son Matthew Garth (Clift). When they separately reach Abilene, Garth with the cattle and Dunson with his gun, they come to blows, then reconcile and join forces as cattlemen with a new brand, which Wayne draws in the dirt. After finishing *Red River*, Hawks presented Wayne with a sterling silver belt buckle crafted in the shape of the brand, which Wayne went on to wear in numerous pictures.

Along with the well-drawn portraits of Dunson and Garth, Hawks's cameras gave an almost documentary quality to the arduous trail drive via lingering close-ups of each of the drovers whooping it up at the drive's onset, contrasted with their beaten exhaustion near its end. Using nine thousand head of cattle, Hawks created a

Trail-worn John Wayne and Montgomery Clift (above) slug it out for pole position in Hawks's *Red River* (1948), a landmark essay in cowboy verismo. Sheriff John T. Chance (Wayne) and young gun Colorado Ryan (Ricky Nelson) take on the bad guys (opposite) in Hawks's *Rio Bravo* (1958). Hawks was so fascinated by the characters in *Rio Bravo* that he went on to produce variations on his theme in *El Dorado* (1967), this time with Wayne as a hired gun and Robert Mitchum as a drunken sheriff (inset).

realistically frightening stampede that reduces the cowhands' numbers.

Ten years on, Hawks made *Rio Bravo*, a completely different type of Western, though the emphasis again is on character development. It was reportedly Hawks's response to *High Noon* (1952), which expressed screenwriter Carl Foreman's anti-McCarthyism. Wayne plays the beleaguered sheriff as the counterpart of *High Noon*'s deserted lawman. In *Rio Bravo*, unlike *High Noon*, the townfolk rally round their lawman to help him beat the marauding killers, but he depends on a few deputies to get the job done. Hawks and Wayne went on to make follow-up films *El Dorado* (1967) and *Rio Lobo* (1971), with similar themes and characters.

IT'S THE BIG ONE WITH THE BIG TWO!

HOWARD HAWKS
presents
JOHN WAYNE
IS THE GUNFIGHTER
ROBERT MITCHUM
IS THE SHERIFF

They were friends. They were enemies. A passerby could not tell which was who.

This was the seething sultry Old Southwest. Where loyalties and labels shifted with the sands, the winking of an eye, the wavering of a gun!

EL DORADO

Mann and the Modern Western

In the 1950s, a new generation of directors started blazing a Western trail, veering off slightly from the footsteps of Ford, Hawks, and King. Anthony Mann, born Emil Bundsmann in 1906, began his career in New York's off-Broadway theater. He came to Hollywood as a casting director for David Selznick. After making several thrillers in the late 1940s, Mann began directing Westerns—the first, *Devil's Doorway* in 1950. He soon carved out a niche for himself as the maker of highly personal Westerns, characterized by panoramic vistas, brutal violence, and well-developed characters. Of the eighteen films he made in the 1950s, eleven were Westerns, eight of them featuring James Stewart.

The Mann hero so often played by Stewart was a conflicted man who doggedly pursued some goal or mission with determination. Usually, he was driven by revenge. As film historian Jim Kitses puts it, "In general all of Mann's heroes behave as if driven by a vengeance they must inflict upon themselves for having once been human, trusting, and therefore, vulnerable. Hence the schizophrenic style of the hero, the violent explosions of passion alternating with precarious moments of quiet reflection." In addition to Stewart, other top actors took on these complicated heroics in Mann films, including Gary Cooper (*Man of the West*), Henry Fonda (*The Tin Star*), Barbara Stanwyck (*The Furies*), and Victor Mature (*The Last Frontier*). The landscape in Mann films is rugged and harsh, which

183

Gilbert Roland and Barbara Stanwyck in *The Furies* (1950), in which Anthony Mann, the director with a fascination for betrayal and revenge, brings a touch of classical Greek tragedy into the genre in his second-ever Western. *The Furies* is, of course, another name for the Eumenides, the relentless bearers of the gods' vengeance.

Mann once said proved a motivating factor for the acting: "A Western is a wonderful thing to do because you take a group of actors who have acted on the stage or who have acted in rooms and now you take them out in the elements and the elements make them much greater as actors than if they were in a room. Because they have to shout above the winds, they have to suffer, they have to climb mountains...." Similarly, Mann uses violent punishment in his films as a kind of Herculean test that the hero must undergo before reaching victory and redemption.

Stewart becomes almost Christlike in *The Man from Laramie*, his hand pierced by short-range gunfire. At the film's climax, the hero climbs the mount to rid it of weaponry used by the Indians to commit the sin of murder.

Mann shifted to directing historical epics in the 1960s. However, at the time of his death, he was planning a return to the West with *The King*, a cowboy version of King Lear. Kitses has compared Mann's legacy with that of Ford: "A rich contrast to

John Ford in many ways, Mann followed the old veteran in the common cause of a visual cinema, pictorial values above all. The kinds of conflict and the terrain itself are vastly different, but the style in both cases unfailingly roots the action in the sweep and pull of landscape. For Ford this broader canvas provided the structure through which he could express his poetic vision of America, in the process carrying on almost single-handedly the romantic mainstream tradition of the genre. For Mann space was cosmic, the camera ever standing back to place his characters in a continuous and elemental reality, Prometheuses chained to their rocks. His contribution was in its way equally unique, the incarnation of his tragic world darkening the genre as no one else has. His neurotic characters and their extraordinary violence were a strange personal gift to the Western, extending its frontiers for both audience and filmmakers that were to follow."

Just as Ford, Hawks, and King brought a durable vision to Westerns in the first half of the 1900s, Mann would influence a new generation of directors making cowboy pictures in the final decades of the twentieth century.

185

Profiteer Emerson Cole (Arthur Kennedy) faces a lynching (opposite) after plotting to steal Oregon pioneers' supplies in Mann's *Bend of the River* (1951), starring James Stewart. In *The Man from Laramie* (above), James Stewart epitomized the complex, vulnerable Mann hero, wounded physically and spiritually. The wound in his hand, an allusion to stigmata, is a clue to the redemptive possibilities inherent in all humanity.

Gene Autry adjusted his successful approach to the small screen by toning down his shirts and cutting down on his singing. The Lone Ranger and his companion Tonto (opposite) made their television debut in 1949, an early instance of the buddy pairing that is now a cliché in most cop shows.

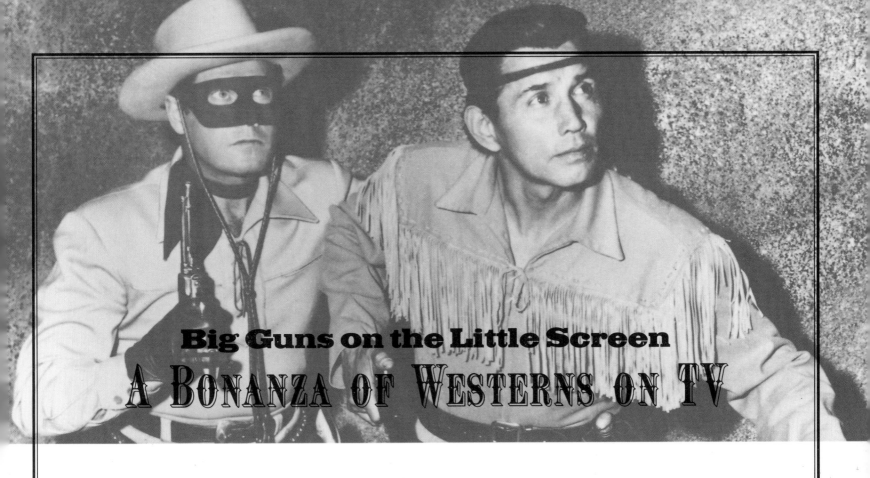

Big Guns on the Little Screen
A Bonanza of Westerns on TV

IN THE EARLY 1950S, WITH THE WANING OF HORSE OPERAS IN MOVIE THEATERS, THERE WAS AN EXPLOSION OF COWBOY PROGRAMS ON TELEVISION. NOT ONLY DID B-MOVIE STARS LIVE ON VIA THEIR OWN TV SHOWS, BUT THERE WAS A SLEW OF NEW PROGRAMMING INSPIRED BY WESTERN MOVIES, BOOKS, RADIO SERIALS, HISTORICAL EVENTS AND FIGURES, AND—OF COURSE—MYTHS.

Hopalong Cassidy, Roy Rogers, and the Lone Ranger

Children were the earliest audience for Westerns on television. The first buckaroo to reach the TV screen was Hopalong Cassidy, when William Boyd sold some of his old movies to some TV stations in Los Angeles and New York in 1945. Audience demand became so great that in 1948 NBC contracted with Boyd to create a half-hour program. Two years later, *Hopalong Cassidy* was the seventh most popular show in the nation. Its vast line of tie-in merchandise, earning Boyd millions of dollars, proved to advertisers the power of television in moving products.

Gene Autry got into television quickly, too. His Flying A Productions created several programs directed toward kids, including 1951's *The Gene*

Autry Show and *The Range Rider*, starring stuntman Jock Mahoney; the 1953 Gail Davis vehicle *Annie Oakley*; and 1955's *The Adventures of Champion* (Autry's horse) and *Buffalo Bill Jr.*, featuring a young buckskin-clad cowpoke (Dick Jones) and his younger sister Calamity. The programs followed the structure developed for Autry's own thirty-minute show: simple plot lines, lots of close-ups, and not much violence or killing.

Roy Rogers and Dale Evans followed a similar model when their show debuted in 1952. Like Autry's program, the show featured less music than in the films. Other popular Western-oriented kiddie programs included *Howdy Doody*, the freckle-faced cowboy puppet, which later inspired the Woody character in the *Toy Story* movies. *Sky King* (1952) starred real-life pilot and former law-enforcement agent Kirby Grant as the Cessna-navigating owner of the Flying Crown Ranch. He and his niece Penny and nephew Clipper are constantly grabbing his plane to fly to the aid of those in need. *Sky King* originated as a Saturday morning radio show in 1946.

Another popular program that began as a radio serial was *The Lone Ranger*. Created in 1933,

Roy Rogers and Dale Evans also made a smooth transition to the smaller screen, introducing a wholesome junior cowboy show that kept the Western myth alive in young hearts.

it featured a do-gooder masked man astride his horse, Silver, accompanied by his Indian pal Tonto. Clayton Moore, who had acted in many B's, starred as TV's Lone Ranger for most of the show's long run from 1949 to 1957 (he left for two years, 1951–1953, over a contract dispute). Jay Silverheels, the Canadian-born son of a Mohawk chief, played Tonto, who rescues the wounded ranger after an ambush, then becomes his faithful companion. The show's famous opener used the musical backdrop of the "William Tell Overture" to add to the drama of the masked man on the rearing Silver, shouting the command, "Hi-yo, Silver, away!" Though that scene was filmed on a picturesque bluff outside Chatsworth, California, the program was primarily shot on a cramped interior set, juxtaposed with old footage of chase scenes used for decades of B's.

Good cop Lone Ranger stands guard while bad cop Tonto gets physical. Few ever asked how a lone ranger could have a constant companion and still describe himself as lone.

Gunsmoke & Adult Westerns

With kids' Westerns like Hopalong Cassidy roping in Mom and Dad as viewers, the networks started developing "adult" cowboy shows for prime-time slots. One of the most popular adult shows of all time, *Gunsmoke* had started out as a successful radio program. It began in 1952 on the radio with William Conrad as Marshal Matt Dillon in the first Western radio serial for adults. Its popularity led to CBS producing it for television beginning in 1955.

The network initially tried to get John Wayne to play Matt Dillon for the TV program. Wayne declined, saying he didn't want to be tied down to a weekly filming schedule. Instead, he recommended a six-foot six-inch actor who was signed to his production company and had played in a few minor films. James Arness, of Norwegian descent, was born James King Aurness in 1923 in Minneapolis. He'd been bumming around California and Mexico after serving in World War II, occasionally acting in theater and B-Westerns, usually as a hulking outlaw. His size helped him get cast in the lead of Howard Hawks's sci-fi thriller, *The Thing* (1951), but no one could see Arness's face thanks to his monster costume.

John Wayne really took to Arness's style and demeanor and gave him a role in his 1952 film *Island in the Sky*, as well as bit parts in *Hondo* and *The Sea Chase*. Reluctant to give up film or to get typecast, Arness originally resisted testing for the *Gunsmoke* role. Wayne encouraged him to go for it, telling him his height would make it difficult for him to get lead roles in the movies. Twenty-six actors tested for the part, including the too-portly Conrad, veterans Randolph Scott and Van Heflin, and even future *Perry Mason* star Raymond Burr, but it went to Arness. As a show of support, Wayne himself made an announcement

Marshal Matt Dillon, the first TV cowboy hero for adults, came with the approval and endorsement of Duke Wayne himself.

GUNSMOKE

FROM THE FAMOUS TELEVISION WESTERN SERIES

introducing the first episode: "I think [*Gunsmoke*] is the best thing of its kind that's come along.... It's honest, it's adult, it's realistic. When I first heard about the show *Gunsmoke*, I knew there was only one man to play in it—James Arness. He's a young fella and maybe new to some of you, but I've worked with him and I predict he'll be a big star. So you might as well get used to him like you've had to get used to me...."

The CBS program first aired as a thirty-minute show on Saturday nights. Arness's costars included Amanda Blake as saloon proprietress Miss Kitty, Dennis Weaver as the comic sidekick Chester Goode, and Milburn Stone as kindly Doc Adams. Rather than focusing on nonstop action and chase scenes, much of the program's emphasis was on interpersonal dramas and relationships. Matt Dillon was no squeaky-clean hero. He drank at Kitty's Long Branch bar, used force when necessary, and violated the unwritten code of the West by sometimes drawing first and even shooting an outlaw in the back. Describing his character,

Arness once said, "Matt is very human and has all the failings and drives common to anyone who is trying to do a difficult job the best he knows how."

During its first year, the program gradually built its popularity until it became an unqualified hit with audiences and advertisers. From its second season until 1965, it ranked in the Nielsen Top 20, taking the first place slot from 1957 to 1961. After six years the show expanded to an hour in length, and both plots and characterization became more complex. Guest stars such as Jon Voigt, Nick Nolte, and Bette Davis, were also featured. In 1967 the show moved to Monday nights and reentered the Nielsen Top 20, where it remained until its last season in 1975—the longest-running Western program of all time.

As well as catapulting Arness to stardom, *Gunsmoke* launched the career of Dennis Weaver, who left in 1964 to play the lead in other television dramas. He was replaced by former singing cowboy and Sons of the Pioneers member Ken Curtis, who became the marshal's humorous buddy Festus.

The *Gunsmoke* ensemble (above), left to right: Miss Kitty and Doc share a joke; Miss Kitty gets uppity; Festus (Feste the clown) the kindly jester, looks up to the marshal, the Duke Orsino of Dodge City; Doc and Miss Kitty pose with Chester, the limping but loyal deputy; Festus; Marshal Matt Dillon.

From Wyatt Earp to Clint Eastwood

The same year *Gunsmoke* debuted, ABC launched two very popular adult programs *The Life and Legend of Wyatt Earp*, starring Hugh O'Brian, and *Cheyenne*, whose six-foot-four-inch star Clint Walker had been a Texas Ranger. Both men found fame through these vehicles, while Westerns began to take over nighttime television. By the 1957–58 season they dominated the ratings, with seven of the Top 10 shows being Westerns. At their peak in 1959, there were nearly fifty prime-time Western programs.

At first, most shows were based on a Western legend (*Bat Masterson, Jim Bowie, Wyatt Earp*), or a loner, roving cowboy (*Bronco, Cheyenne, Have Gun, Will Travel, The Rebel*), or a historical Western town with a fictional sheriff hero (*Gunsmoke, Lawman, The Rifleman*). However, one of the best and most enduring programs didn't really fit into any of those categories. *Wagon Train*, which debuted in 1957 as a one-hour program on NBC, starred John Ford–regular Ward Bond as the wagon master. Each week high-caliber guest stars, among them Barbara Stanwyck, Ernest Borgnine, and Linda Darnell, joined the wagon trail; the drama revolved around these new introductions. The well-written program engaged John Ford as director for one episode; his film *Wagonmaster* was clearly the inspiration for the program. When Bond died in 1961, John McIntire came on as wagonmaster, alongside regulars Terry Wilson as driver Bill Hawks and Frank McGrath as humorous trail cook Charlie Wooster.

Henry Fonda, also attracted to the small screen, took on the role of Marshal Fry in *Deputy*, which ran from 1959 to 1961. As Western movie vets like Fonda and Bond found work in television, some Western movies were transformed into television programs. Delmer Daves's groundbreaking pro-Indian film *Broken Arrow* (1950) became a weekly TV show in 1958, based on the same novel, *Blood Brothers*. It centered around the characters of Cochise and Indian agent Tom Jeffords.

As well as providing work for veterans of cowboy movies and keeping alive past movies, the vast range of Western programming also became the proving ground for several of the genre's future stars. Director Sam Peckinpah started his career as a writer for several Western TV shows, including *Broken Arrow*, *The Westerner*, *Gunsmoke*, and *The Rifleman*. When he started directing movies in the early 1960s, Peckinpah would take the Western into exciting new directions.

Many future movie stars rose from the ranks of Westerns, including Roger Moore, Burt Reynolds, Steve McQueen, James Garner, and Clint Eastwood—the actor who would transform the Western in the 1960s. Eastwood played Rowdy Yates in the cattle drive–based show *Rawhide*, which debuted in 1959.

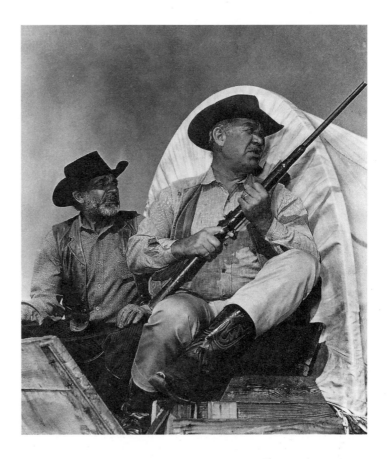

193

Born in San Francisco in 1930, the lean and lanky Eastwood had worked as a lumberjack, gas station attendant, and swimming pool digger before trying acting. He got a contract with Universal in 1954 and was cast in a few bit parts, including one in a Francis the talking mule movie, then landed the role of Rowdy. As right-hand man to trail boss Gil Favor (Eric Fleming), Eastwood became a heartthrob. He even recorded an album for Cameo-Parkway; it bombed. However, Rawhide's theme song, sung by Frankie Laine, became a huge hit.

Some shows presented antiheroes who did not follow the code of the West but acted only from self-interest. The wryly humorous *Maverick*, starring James Garner as callous gambler Bret Maverick, featured a rather cowardly *continued on page 196*

Hugh O'Brian as Wyatt Earp (opposite), following the sartorial standard to which all celluloid Earps subscribed. Original wagonmaster Ward Bond (above) gets ready to roll 'em out in the phenomenally successful *Wagon Train*, the mobile soap opera set on the Oregon Trail. With him is Charlie Wooster, the train's culinary genius. The Cartwright boys (following pages) gather around the *Bonanza* breakfast table in the first Western series to be shown in color.

protagonist who would rather run than fight. Paladin (Richard Boone) was a sophisticated, black-clad hired gun on *Have Gun Will Travel*. Steve McQueen starred as cool, calm, and collected bounty hunter Josh Randall in *Wanted: Dead or Alive*.

By 1960, though cigarette advertisers loved Westerns and got their stars to endorse their brands, critics started harping about the violence and its ill effects on children. The debate grew heated. Congressional hearings were held, and the surgeon general announced that there was a relationship between violence on the tube and violence in real life. Some critics blamed Westerns for setting a bad example regarding violence and gunplay, others argued that the black and white morality plays illustrated the difference between right and wrong and demonstrated that the bad guy always lost—albeit violently. No one really won the argument, but the networks started making other kinds of shows and downplaying violence in the Westerns.

Sugarfoot, for example, told the tale of a pacifist law student cowpoke, played by Will Hutchins, who shunned violence. One of the major new shows was based on a well-to-do ranch

family, with a kindly father figure. *Bonanza* became the second most durable Western after *Gunsmoke*, first airing in 1959 and running for fourteen and a half years—until 1973. Centered around the deep-voiced silver-haired daddy Ben Cartwright (Canadian-born Lorne Greene), the program's plots primarily concerned the various comings and goings of

his three sons, by three different wives: the hefty Hoss (Dan Blocker), handsome Adam (Pernell Roberts), and teen idol Little Joe (Michael Landon). *Bonanza* was the first television Western to be shown in color (the show's popularity may have helped spur the sales of color television sets) and featured the gorgeous scenery of the Cartwrights' sprawling ranch.

Other family shows followed, most prominently the Barbara Stanwyck vehicle *The Big Valley*. Stanwyck had been trying to land a Western television program since the mid-1950s, but only after *Bonanza*'s success did she get the green light. As the widow Victoria Barkley, she ruled the Barkley family ranch with a toughness that equaled Ben Cartwright's. Dramas involved her

The Wild Wild West (above and background) starring Robert Conrad as James T. West, Ross Martin as his partner Artemus Gordon, and a changing roster of distressed lovelies, was a psychedelic amalgam of spies, cowboys, fantasy, and martial arts set in the 1870s. It could only have been made in the 1960s, and ran from 1965 to 1969, when it was axed because it was considered too violent. Will Smith and Kevin Kline starred in the 1999 big-screen version. Barbara Stanwyck (opposite, left) as Victoria Barkley sits down to stand up to the men in her life in *The Big Valley*, the first and only Western series built around a strong female character. Jane Seymour is the unlikely Dr. Quinn, Medicine Woman (opposite, center). James Garner as Bret Maverick (opposite, right), the smooth-talking con artist who just knew that a dude and his money are soon parted.

grown children, Jarrod (Richard Long), Audra (Linda Evans), Nick (Peter Breck), and Eugene (Charles Briles). Heath (Lee Majors) was the offspring of a liaison between Barkley's husband and a Native American woman; apparently Stanwyck wanted the character to be her own illegitimate child, but the network found the idea too risqué. Airing from 1965 to 1969, the program was the first adult Western to star a woman.

By the mid-1960s, though, Westerns were running out of steam on television. Only one new show enjoyed the vast popularity that *Gunsmoke* and *Bonanza* had attracted: *The Virginian*, starring James Drury in the title role, was the first TV Western to run for ninety minutes. Debuting in 1962, it starred Lee J. Cobb and Doug McClure, along with numerous guests.

The Virginian went off the air in 1971 while it was still popular. By the 1970s demographics had become more important to the networks than the number of viewers. When it was discovered that *The Virginian*'s audience—and likewise the audience for other Westerns—was more rural, working-class, and younger or older than the middle-aged, affluent, urban audience sought by advertisers, the networks

started taking the shows off the air. A few programs with new angles were added to attract a more desirable viewership, including the cowboy-meets-James Bond-style thriller *The Wild Wild West,* the cavalry sitcom *F Troop*, and the wronged outlaw-buddy drama *Alias Smith and Jones*.

Westerns have never actually vanished from television. They continue in reruns and in syndication on late-night TV. Occasionally television programs with Western themes—such as *Dr. Quinn, Medicine Woman* and *Walker, Texas Ranger*, which debuted in 1993—and critically and commercially successful miniseries—such as the Larry McMurtry novel *Lonesome Dove* (1989) and its 1993 sequel, *Return to Lonesome Dove*—have found huge audiences. With the proliferation of channels on cable and satellite television, reruns of Western programs have now returned in force. By the late 1990s there was an entire channel devoted to them. The Western Channel runs the West and nothing but the West, from major feature films to the 1950s television programs for kids to the classic adult Westerns of the 1950s and 1960s. Though television is by no means as saturated with the cowboy as it once was, it's still unlikely that the Western TV show will ever ride off into the sunset for good.

198

Clint Eastwood is the man with no name (above), the new icon of the West. *The Magnificent Seven* (opposite) made avenging angels out of gunslinging mercenaries.

The Good, the Bad, and the Ugly Meet the Wild Bunch
LEONE, PECKINPAH, EASTWOOD, AND THE ANTICOWBOY

IN THE 1960S A NEW KIND OF WESTERN FEATURING A NEW KIND OF COWBOY— MORE GUNMAN THAN CATTLEMAN— CAME TO DOMINATE THE SCREEN. DIRECTORS SERGIO LEONE AND SAM PECKINPAH AND ACTOR CLINT EASTWOOD BROUGHT ABOUT A RESURGENCE IN WESTERNS CHARACTERIZED BY GRITTY, IN-YOUR-FACE VIOLENCE, DOWN 'N' DIRTY COSTUMING, AND AN IRONIC, CYNICAL TONE.

As the making of Hollywood Westerns ebbed in the late 1950s, Westerns showed no signs of abating overseas, which actually helped to infuse the American market with new ideas. The masterful Japanese director Akira Kurosawa modeled his landmark film *The Seven Samurai* after a classic Western drama. He commented, "Westerns have been made over and over again, and in the process a kind of grammar has evolved. I have learned from this grammar of the Western." In America in 1960, director John Sturges then took Kurosawa's film and adapted it into *The Magnificent Seven*. Centering around a septet of killers hired to protect a Mexican village from a local bandito (Eli Wallach) and his gang, the film starred a mixed bag of actors. Some of them went on to become the new action heroes of Westerns, as well as of later spy and crime dramas: Steve McQueen, James Coburn, Charles Bronson, and Robert Vaughan. The film

was influential in other ways: its theme of a cowboy elite hired to get the job done became popular, not only in the three *Magnificent Seven* sequels but in other films, and its Elmer Bernstein theme song was picked up by Marlboro to accompany cigarette-smoking buckaroos riding the range on TV commercials.

In Italy, director Sergio Leone—a lifelong Western fan who had assisted on several American film productions in Europe—began work in 1964 on an action-packed shoot-'em-up of his own. Proving there was a European market, German producers had recently struck gold with a series of films based on Karl May's frontier novels (similar to James Fenimore Cooper's *Leatherstocking Tales*), which starred imported American actor Lex Barker. A limited budget killed Leone's dream of casting Henry Fonda or James Coburn in the lead for his debut Western, so he settled on *Rawhide*'s Clint Eastwood. Eastwood had been champing at the bit to make films, but his CBS television contract prevented him from doing so in the States. The ten features he'd been in before *Rawhide* amounted to mostly bit parts, so the thirty-seven-year-old Eastwood gladly accepted an

offer of $15,000 and welcomed the chance to spend his summer break in Europe.

Thus began a transformation of Eastwood's clean-cut, grinning Rowdy Yates character into a glinty-eyed, terse-lipped, stubble-chinned, cigarillo-smoking anticowboy. The German–Italian coproduction filmed in Spain, originally titled *The Magnificent Stranger*, was based on another Kurosawa film, *Yojimbo* (which was inspired in part by *Shane*). In Leone's picture, Eastwood's scruffy Stranger, garbed in dark poncho, beat-up flat-brimmed hat, and dusty skintight jeans, comes sauntering into the Mexican village of San Miguel astride a mule. After being shot at by one group of thugs, he observes another nasty crew firing at a toddler scampering in the street. Deciding to take advantage of the two viciously competitive families seeking to control the godforsaken place, the cold-blooded, sharpshooting Stranger hatches a plan by hiring himself out to each clan as a mercenary. An unprecedented filmic brutality follows, characterized by a kind of choreographed gorefest juxtaposed with lingering close-ups of leering desperadoes. At one point, the Stranger's face becomes a hideous Quasimodo

Who would have thought that fresh-faced young Rowdy Yates, *Rawhide*'s babe magnet, seen here (left) with trail boss Gil Favor (Eric Fleming), would have gone to the dark side for just a fistful of dollars? But he did.

Yul Brynner and six other magnificos line up to defend the town (background). Brynner later reprised his implacable avenger, this time as an android in Michael Crichton's Western sci-fi fantasy *Westworld* (1973). The poncho, a hitherto neglected fashion item, becomes a style icon (inset), sartorial shorthand for a whole new genre.

One of the uglier scenes (following pages) from Sergio Leone's *The Good, The Bad, and the Ugly* (1966), a timeless narrative of three desperadoes and a heap of hidden treasure.

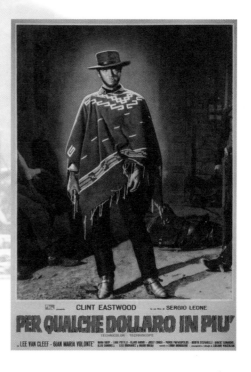

201

monstrosity after a sadistic beating. The Stranger's amoral stance and qualms-free precision with his pistol, as well as his low-key, withdrawn demeanor, created a new kind of antiheroic icon. Eastwood's soft-spoken, gruff delivery and granite-faced resolve contrasted greatly with the overemoting, flamboyant acting of the Italians—what Eastwood has called the "hellzapoppin' school of drama."

In Italy, violence wasn't subjected to the same scrutiny by film censors as in the States. The Hays Commission had traditionally restricted American productions from showing in a single frame the act of a gun being fired and the bullet striking a victim. "You had to shoot separately, and then show the person fall," Eastwood told Leone biographer Christopher Frayling. "And that was always thought sort of stupid. But on television we always did it that way.... And you see, Sergio never knew that."

Leone attributed his bloody denouements to his desire to recreate the real West, as well as his background acting in and assisting on films by Italian neorealists such as Vittorio De Sica (*The Bicycle Thief*). "I love the authentic when it is filtered through imagination, myth, mystery and poetry," he once said. "But it is essential that, at base, all the details seem right.... This fusion of reality and fantasy takes us into a different dimension—of myth, of legend."

Adding to the visceral package was Ennio Morricone's evocative sound track. It combined Latin-tinged melodies with exotic instrumentation, including the Sicilian *guimbard*, the North African *maranzano*, and the flute, along with whip cracks, whistling, and guttural chanting. Morricone later described working closely with Leone on the music to "complete certain characters continued on page 204

on the screen, to complete them as types.... I wanted to hammer out a kind of music which was more pressing, more troubled, more of a direct experience." Upon its release, the film became enormously successful in Italy. However, due to a lawsuit between Leone and Kurosawa, it was not released in the States until 1967. It then appeared with the title *A Fistful of Dollars*; Eastwood's character was referred to as "The Man With No Name," and Leone's name in the credits was listed as "Bob Robertson."

In 1965, Leone set to work on a sequel, this time pairing Eastwood with another little-known American actor, Lee Van Cleef. Van Cleef had played the heavy in a number of Westerns, including *High Noon*, *Gunfight at the O.K. Corral*, and *The Bravados*. When cast by Leone, he'd given up acting for painting after being seriously injured in a car accident. In *A Few Dollars More*, Eastwood and Van Cleef played conniving, brutal bounty hunters vying for the same mark—the pot-smoking, murderous bandito Indio, who rapes and pillages in drug-crazed frenzies. Van Cleef's role as the snake-eyed, sneering killer Colonel Mortimer resulted in his becoming a superstar in Europe, acting in twelve Westerns over the next nine years.

Leone's next project, *The Good, the Bad, and the Ugly*, teamed Van Cleef and Eastwood with scene-stealing Method actor Eli Wallach, who had played the killer bandit in *The Magnificent Seven*. All three are in search of gold treasure hidden by Confederate soldiers, with the raging Civil War adding a bloody backdrop to the plot. This film had more liberal doses of Leone's earthy—sometimes gross-out—humor, which was hinted at in the first two films. Morricone contributed his most famous sound track of all, with a moody but catchy theme song that became a classic. The 1967 album made the American pop charts, where it stayed for a year, peaking at number four.

That same year, all three films were finally released in the States, inaugurating the term "spaghetti Western." They became hugely popular with audiences but received a negative reaction from the press and from some directors associated with the Western, among them John Ford, Anthony Mann, and Budd Boetticher. Mann later complained that "the true spirit of the Western is lacking [in *For a Few Dollars More*]. We tell the story of simple men pushed to violence by circumstances...not of professional assassins. In a good Western, the characters have a starting and a finishing line; they follow a trajectory in the course of which they clash with life. The characters in *A Few Dollars More* meet along their road only the 'black' of life."

But Leone continued to persist in his own singular vision of the West, which paid homage to the masters of the medium while putting his own unique—albeit bloody—stamp on them. He reached his apotheosis with his next effort, 1968's *Once Upon a Time in the West*. This time he had the stature and financing to film part of the movie in the legendary Monument Valley, where his hero John Ford had shot so many pictures. In his twisted way, though, Leone cast the typically white-hatted Henry Fonda as the despicable killer, Frank, and Charles Bronson as the "good guy," Harmonica, in his first-ever starring role. Leone later said the film was comprised of "quotes from all the Westerns I love." Indeed, visual, thematic, and/or character references can be found from *High Noon*, *Johnny Guitar*, *Shane*, *The Iron Horse*, *The Searchers*, and *Winchester '73*, among others. The ambitious film failed at the box office, however. After next shooting the Mafia epic *Once Upon a Time in America*, Leone directed only one more Western. His 1971 picture *A Fistful of Dynamite*, originally saddled with the bizarre title *Duck You Sucker*, also fared poorly.

A Fistful of Dollars (1964) is the first of the spaghetti Westerns featuring the stranger from the dark side, amoral and therefore endlessly fascinating to all those who want to redeem his soul.

★ PECKINPAH'S VIOLENT WEST ★

Negative reactions in the States to Leone's films focused on the intense violence and the lack of motivation shown for the characters' sadistic behavior. In the meantime, American director Sam Peckinpah had been moving in a similar direction. His brilliant 1962 picture *Ride the High Country*, starring Randolph Scott and Joel McCrea, was populated with savage characters who abuse women and double-cross and brutalize each other. There was still a sort of moral sanctity, though, in the characters played by McCrea and Scott, a pair of aging cowhands trying to hold on to their dignity. Peckinpah's 1969 tour de force, *The Wild Bunch*, was much more ambiguous—and more of a bloodfest. From its ominous opening credits shots of scorpions

being destroyed by swarming ants while laughing children watch, there's no distinguishing the good guys from the bad guys in this film. *The Wild Bunch*, based loosely on Butch Cassidy, the Sundance Kid, and the Hole in the Wall gang—played by William Holden (as the leader Pike Bishop), Ernest Borgnine, Warren Oates, and Ben Johnson—ride into town disguised as an army unit. Their plan to rob a train depot is foiled by an ambush by a savage gang of raggle-taggle bounty hunters, led by Thornton (Robert Ryan), a former Wild Bunch member who has been imprisoned and coerced into participating. Fifteen minutes of carnage follow, accentuated by slow motion artfully choreographed camera movement and close-ups of the slaughter of

Temperance League bystanders—with women and children numbering among the bullet-riddled victims. A chase into Mexico ensues, climaxing in a nihilistic show of bad-guy heroics when the Bunch returns to a corrupt Mexican village to destroy the sadistic General Mapache and his henchmen who'd hired them to pull a weaponry heist from the U.S. Army. In one particularly spectacular scene, a bridge being crossed by the bounty hunters is blown up, with horses, men, and equipment exploding into the air and falling into the river below. After another long, explicitly gory shoot-out—this time with a primitive machine gun as a centerpiece—just about everyone in the film except for Thornton is butchered.

In addition to its moral ambiguity, *The Wild Bunch* broke down barriers in American filmmaking with regard to the amount of graphic violence and fire power shown on the screen. Peckinpah became renowned—and in some quarters vilified—for such blood 'n' guts moviemaking. "*The Wild Bunch* became a kind of paean to violence," was the viewpoint of Western historian William Everson, "and neither the pious pronouncements of its stars and director that it had to depict violence graphically in order to condemn it, nor the unquestioned

virtuosity of its pictorial style (slaughter scenes and moments of excessively detailed bloodletting presented in slow motion to create an effect of choreography and ritual) could really counter or justify the effect of revulsion and nausea that it created." Offering the converse opinion, however, was Western critic Jon Tuska, who wrote, "What Sam...achieve[d] was to make a poetry of violence, to show the anguished features it wears in men who are weary of having to live with it and who no longer know how to contend with its importunities."

In the 1970s, Peckinpah focused on the extinction of the cowboy lifestyle in several films in which the violence was toned down somewhat. *The Ballad of Cable Hogue* (1970) featured Jason Robards as an unscrupulous desert dweller who operates a stagecoach stop but gets run down by a newfangled automobile. *Junior Bonner* (1972), a contemporary

Western, starred the cool, laconic Steve McQueen as a down-on-his-luck former rodeo star. In 1973, Peckinpah returned to outlaws with the somewhat surrealistic *Pat Garrett and Billy the Kid*. With hunky Kris Kristofferson as Billy and sly James Coburn as Pat Garrett, the film was a sort of counterculture Western, featuring iconic Bob Dylan as the vague commentator Alias and Native American singer Rita Coolidge as Billy's girlfriend, as well as Jason Robards and Katy Jurado (*High Noon*) and a slew of traditional Western character actors, including Slim Pickens, Jack Elam, Chill Wills, Dub Taylor, and L. Q. Jones. Dylan's evocative sound track for the film yielded one of his most eloquent, enduring compositions, "Knockin' on Heaven's Door." The elegiac, moodily beautiful film seemed to bid farewell to the Wild West as the Kid, who refuses to give up the archaic outlaw ways, is shot dead by Garrett, his old friend who has adapted to societal changes. Peckinpah, who claimed to reporters that he hadn't been sober in twenty years, said during filming, "Unless you conform, give in completely, you're going to be alone in this world. But by giving in, you lose your independence as a human being. So I go for the losers on a grand scale as well as a kind of sneaky affection for all the misfits and drifters in the world."

207

Sam Peckinpah's *Wild Bunch* (opposite) hit town in 1969 to show in shocking slow motion what really happens when lead rips through flesh. Kris Kristofferson is Billy the Kid (above) in Peckinpah's take on the enduring legend, with Kid fan Bob Dylan providing the requiem sound track.

EASTWOOD IN AMERICA

Meanwhile, *Rawhide* had been canceled after a seven-year run and Clint Eastwood's star had risen thanks to the Leone films. In 1968, Eastwood's first American-made Western, *Hang 'Em High*, picked up where The Man With No Name left off. It opened with what would become a signature for Eastwood's American films, a brief introductory scene showing an innocent man being victimized—documenting the reason behind his becoming a vengeful killer. In *Hang 'Em High*, Eastwood's character Cooper is seen gently rescuing a calf from a pond, when he is mistaken by a band of vigilantes for a murderous cattle rustler. The men brutally hang him—an event shown in all its excruciating graphic detail. A passing marshal (Ben Johnson) rescues Cooper, who, after being cleared of the charges, becomes a marshal working under the jurisdiction of Judge Fenton. Fenton's character was based on the real-life "hanging judge" Isaac Parker who in the 1870s built a public gallows that could accommodate twelve men. Cooper hunts down the nine who tried to kill him, but eventually shows more compassion than the Judge. The film gave a nod to William Wellman's dark 1942 Western *The Ox-Bow Incident*, in which three innocent men are lynched by a group of vigilantes, among them a cowhand played with a quiet intensity by Henry Fonda. An indictment of the mob mentality of the anti-Communist Red Scare, the psychological drama had the residual effect of illustrating the moral ambiguity of Western "justice," a theme that gradually picked up steam in films made over the next decades.

In his American movies, Eastwood continued to develop his taciturn Western character with his signature raspy whisper (reportedly inspired by Marilyn Monroe's sexy murmur) and unflinching "eye for an eye" retaliatory violence, no matter the

Coogan's Bluff (1968) saw Eastwood bring the West to a contemporary setting (left). It marked his emergence from screen anonymity and laid a dirt trail to maverick cop Harry Callahan. Bulk dispatch in *Hang 'Em High* (opposite, directed by Ted Post, 1967), Eastwood's first Western after returning to the United States.

consequences. He left behind in Spain, however, the little Italian stogies Leone had his Man With No Name constantly smoking. Eastwood reportedly detested the hard-to-light, potent cigarillos. Leone liked to tell the story that when Eastwood tried to dispense with them, the director told him, "But, Clint, the cigar is playing the lead!" Eastwood kept several stogies of various lengths on the set so he didn't have to actually take a drag on them, though he later pointed to one benefit of smoking the foul things: "If I had to be in an unpleasant frame of mind, I took a couple of draws and, boy, I was right there."

In the late 1960s, Eastwood began zigzagging between Westerns and contemporary police dramas, beginning with *Coogan's Bluff* (1968), directed by Don Siegel. In it, he plays a contemporary range-riding sheriff from Arizona who travels to New York City to bag a crook. In 1971, the Eastwood–Siegel collaborations moved into a series of Dirty Harry films, starring Eastwood as the bad-ass San Francisco detective who coined the phrase "make my day" while aiming his Magnum .44. A 1971 cover story in *Life*

magazine condescendingly quoted Eastwood's detractors, "It has been said that Clint Eastwood learned to act at the Mount Rushmore Dramatic Academy," while pointing out that he was number two at the box office (after Paul Newman) and that his films to date had grossed close to $200 million.

Eastwood's Malapo Productions financed and produced his films. In 1976 he directed the richly textured and compelling picture *The Outlaw Josey Wales*. A hardworking farmer, Wales loses his wife and child to a brutal Yankee gang during the Civil War. He spends the film seeking revenge and living on the lam, assembling his own pseudo "family" in the process. Beautifully photographed and well-acted, featuring Sondra Locke and Chief Dan George, the film began to win Eastwood favorable notices as a director. It was a sign of things to come for Eastwood. In the 1990s he would be fêted for his artistic vision of the West, but unfortunately those hard-living men who had helped pave the way wouldn't be around to see it: Sam Peckinpah died in 1984 at age fifty-nine, Leone in 1989, aged sixty.

Definitely not bluffing; Walt Coogan (left) kicks face in the celebrated poolroom fight scene from Don Siegel's first movie with Clint Eastwood. Eastwood (above) directed and starred in *The Outlaw Josey Wales* (1976) to impressive effect. A decade on from his spaghetti years, to his public he was still the enigmatic loner.

Misfits, Young Riders, and "Unforgiven"
THE REVISIONIST OLD AND NEW WEST

FOR THE MOST PART, AS THE TWENTIETH CENTURY NEARED ITS CLOSE, THE WESTERN AS A COHESIVE GENRE SEEMED TO BE REACHING THE END OF ITS ROPE. THEMATICALLY, IT WAS ALL OVER THE MAP, AND ITS MAJOR ACTORS AND DIRECTORS WERE RETIRED OR DEAD. NEW, REVISIONIST WESTERNS FOR THE FIRST TIME OFFERED STRONG ROLES FOR WOMEN AND PEOPLE OF COLOR.

They told the Western story from the Native American perspective and showed a heightened concern for the environment. Overall, there was a renewed interest in historical accuracy as a new generation of players endeavored to take cowboys into the next millennium.

The Western's new concerns had precedents dating back to the 1950s, when films began exploring the changing lifestyle of contemporary cowboys. Even in the 1930s there was an element of this, as when Gene Autry fought speakeasy gangsters who sped away in modern roadsters. In these new Westerns, however, contemporary cowboys struggled to survive in the modern world while living by their old codes. Sometimes they succeed by adapting, as in George Stevens's 1956 epic *Giant*, based on the Edna Ferber novel. Ranch owner Jordan Benedict (Rock Hudson) sees the old Texas cattle-raising

ou never met pair like Butch nd The Kid

They're Taking Trains... They're Taking Banks And They're Taking One Piece Of Baggage!

Kevin Costner in the surprise blockbuster *Dances with Wolves* (overleaf) (1992). *Pale Rider* (1985), Clint Eastwood's self-directed version of *Shane* (opposite), did not fare well at the box office—perhaps the public had had it with taciturn avengers.

Butch and Sundance (opposite) reach the end of the line in a Bolivian hacienda; or do they? George Roy Hill's celebratory biopic leaves the end ambivalent, unwilling to administer the *coup de grâce* to its likable heroes. Richard Farnsworth (below) growing old gracefully in the saddle in 1982's *The Grey Fox*, directed by Phillip Borsos.

lifestyle slipping away as it is taken over by vast oil-digging enterprises operated by nouveau riche tycoons. Along with Hudson, Elizabeth Taylor, James Dean, and Mercedes McCambridge, the cast included a cavalcade of actors who had made their mark in Westerns—Monte Hale, Chill Wills, Sheb Wooley, Ray Whitley, and Max Terhune among them.

In Arthur Miller's brilliant and moving Marilyn Monroe vehicle, *The Misfits*, aging rodeo cowboys—Eli Wallach and Clark Gable, in his last film—try to maintain their old livelihood by lassoing wild horses to be turned into dog food. This theme was elaborated on in George Roy Hill's *Butch Cassidy and the Sundance Kid*, in which Butch (Paul Newman) and Sundance (Robert Redford), unable to continue robbing trains in America, must relocate to Bolivia to continue their outlaw lifestyle.

One of the most successful films of 1969, it yielded a hit song with Burt Bacharach's "Raindrops Keep Falling on My Head," performed by B. J. Thomas.

Another bittersweet look at the Old West was Robert Altman's moody *McCabe and Mrs. Miller* (1971), which finds two-bit entrepreneur McCabe (Warren Beatty) unable to survive when the mining town he helped to create becomes "civilized," while brothel madam Mrs. Miller (Julie Christie) escapes through opium addiction. The gorgeous Leonard Cohen sound track added even more of a melancholy flavor to the film. The beautifully photographed, elegiac Western *The Grey Fox* (1983) starred septuagenarian Richard Farnsworth, who had acted in silent Westerns, as an elderly cowhand witnessing the end of the Western frontier while finding a new life with a liberated female photographer.

THE WESTERN'S LOW EBB

By the late 1980s, though, Westerns had fallen on hard times, becoming fewer and fewer in number. The decade started with a sort of scaled-down *Magnificent Seven*–style action picture, 1980's *The Long Riders*, directed by Walter Hill. Real-life brothers play outlaw siblings: David, Keith, and Robert Carradine as the Youngers, Stacy and James Keach as the Jameses, Dennis and Randy Quaid as the James gang's Miller brothers, and Christopher and Nicholas Guest as the Jesse–killing Ford brothers. It spawned a craze for dusters, but didn't do particularly well at the box office.

Casting a pall over the entire decade was the film many pundits say killed off the Western. Michael Cimino's long-awaited follow-up to his brilliant Vietnam film *The Deer Hunter* also arrived in 1980. *Heaven's Gate* marked a return to the Western epic but was a complete critical and commercial failure. Costing $36 million, it originally clocked in at over 200 minutes but fared no better after being trimmed to 149 minutes. It even

seemed to scare off Clint Eastwood, who only did one Western film in that decade, 1985's *Pale Rider*, which made a rather lackluster showing at the box office. That year's *Silverado*, a homesteaders versus cattlemen drama directed by Lawrence Kasdan, did not make much of an impact either.

In 1988, the Brat Pack (the ironically nicknamed eighties answer to the Rat Pack) showed an interest in the Western with *Young Guns*. It starred Emilio Estevez as Billy the Kid and Charlie Sheen, Lou Diamond Phillips, and Kiefer Sutherland as his companions in the Lincoln County War. This turned into a 1989–1992 television series, *Young Riders*, and spawned a sequel in 1990, *Young Guns II*. Showing how far expectations had fallen for "Western" actors, the packaging for the video of the picture boasted, "During the course of filming, all the actors became accomplished riders, practiced gun-twirling, knife-throwing and falling backward off horses until it seemed like second nature."

In 1992 the resurgence of the Western and the primacy of the revisionist Western began with the release of *Dances with Wolves*, produced and directed by Kevin Costner. Costner plays cavalry officer Lt. John Dunbar, who is given a lonely outpost near a Sioux encampment. The painstakingly politically correct film, several years in the making, features the Lakota language (with subtitles in English) and paints a respectful portrait of the Sioux' harmonious coexistence with nature. The Native American culture is shown to be far superior to the corrupt "civilized" one from which Dunbar hails. He and his Sioux neighbors come to understand and respect one another as brothers, and he marries a white woman raised by the tribe. Winning seven Academy Awards, including best picture, the film set off a new craze for Westerns.

Thematically, *Dances with Wolves* did have a few filmic predecessors, from sentimental silent films *The Squaw Man* (1918) and *The Vanishing American* (1926) to Delmer Daves's *Broken Arrow* (1950), John Ford's *Cheyenne Autumn* (1964), Arthur Penn's *Little Big Man* (1970), starring Dustin Hoffman, and *Soldier Blue* (1972), featuring Candice Bergen, which conveyed the horrific slaughter of the Cheyenne at the Sand Creek Massacre.

For his film, Costner enlisted Native Americans as technical advisors on Sioux culture. The carefully made and historically accurate *Dances with Wolves* cast Native American actors who spoke the tribal language; in the past, Native Americans had been played by white actors, including Rock Hudson, Debra Paget, and Jeff Chandler. Walter Hill likewise took care to include Native Americans as advisors and actors in his 1993 biopic, *Geronimo: An American Legend*, but it failed to generate the same excitement among audiences.

The Long Riders (1980), directed by gangsta-loving Walter Hill (opposite, left), was a stylishly violent presentation of the Jesse James story featuring a slew of Hollywood brothers in starring roles. The 1980s Brat Pack (opposite, right) took on Billy the Kid in *Young Guns* (1988), directed by Christopher Cain. Its Billy, 25-year-old Emilio Estevez, at least shared an age group with the original, who was dead before he was 24. A characteristically overambitious scene (opposite, center) from Michael Cimino's *Heaven's Gate*, considered by some to be a fatal wound to the Western genre. The single-handed sincerity of Kevin Costner's *Dances with Wolves* (background), in which the Indian side of the Western myth is examined in detail, struck a chord with audiences and rekindled interest in the American past.

218

Women, whose point of view and accurate portrayal had been ignored by traditional Westerns, also got their say in the 1990s in films such as 1994's *Bad Girls*, featuring a gang of female outlaws; 1993's *The Ballad of Little Jo*, a well-made drama based on the true story of Jo Monaghan; and the Sharon Stone vehicle *The Quick and the Dead*, which also starred Gene Hackman as her adversary and Leonardo DiCaprio as the archetypal Kid gunslinger. The predecessor to the latter dates back to 1972, with the Peckinpah–inspired, Burt Kennedy–directed *Hannie Caulder*. In that movie, a vengeful Raquel Welch gets shooting lessons from a bounty hunter (Robert Culp) to go on a bloodthirsty rampage against the three desperadoes, played by Western baddies Ernest Borgnine, Jack Elam, and Strother Martin, who had raped her and killed her husband.

The Latin experience has also been expressed in more positive ways in 1990s Westerns. A native of Spain, Antonio Banderas returned the dashing masked crusader to the screen in *The Mask of Zorro*, and Robert Rodriguez created a new series of action films with his *Desperado* series.

African-American actors were featured more frequently in Westerns, beginning in such Eastwood films as *Hang 'Em High*. Mario Van Peebles's 1993 effort, *Posse*, was a strong action Western featuring a predominantly black cast.

One of the Western's most popular subjects, the shoot-out at the O.K. Corral, was the focus of a concurrent pair of movies that were made in the early 1990s. Each one, of course, claimed to be the definitive accounting: 1993's *Tombstone*, starring Val Kilmer (Doc Holliday) and Kurt Russell (Wyatt Earp), and *Wyatt Earp* starring Kevin Costner (Earp) and Dennis Quaid (Holliday). Buffalo Bill came under scrutiny once again in *Buffalo Gals*, based on the Larry McMurtry novel, and starring Angelica Huston as Calamity Jane and Reba McEntire as Annie Oakley.

Attempts to cash in on the Western's renewed popularity were characterized by several "remakes" of popular 1960s television series. James Garner's humorous *Maverick* became a clunky motion picture starring Mel Gibson and Jodie Foster, with Garner getting a

cameo role. Though Will Smith was an interesting casting choice for James West, the remake of *The Wild Wild West* was also a dud.

Filmmakers did much better when presenting fresh new ideas about the contemporary West. Highlights include a modern-day "dudes-go-West" picture, Billy Crystal's comical *City Slickers*, which featured an Oscar-winning performance by Jack Palance as the kind of frightening gun-toting buckaroo that he created in the chilling gunslinger in *Shane*. Other standouts include a new kind of "cowgirl" action picture, *Thelma and Louise*, and an exploration of the Mexico–Texas border difficulties in John Sayles's superb *Lone Star*. The rodeo cowboy lifestyle, so well depicted by Peckinpah in *Junior Bonner*, got a worthwhile portrayal by Eastwood in 1980's *Bronco Billy*, and was taken into the honky-tonks by *Urban Cowboy*, which set off an unprecedented mechanical bull–riding craze. The more recent *8½ Seconds*, a biopic of the doomed rodeo star Lane Cross, did not do much for Luke Perry's post–*Beverly Hills 90210* career, however, nor did it boost entrants into the Pro Rodeo League. Another former television heartthrob—Johnny Depp—made a much more stirring appearance in Jim Jarmusch's artful *Dead Man*, a quirky exploration of Western mythmaking that also had something to say about ecological issues—all to the accompaniment of a Neil Young sound track.

Without a doubt, though, the most successful, innovative, emotionally compelling, and action-packed Western of the 1990s belongs to Clint Eastwood. His 1992 masterpiece *Unforgiven* capped his career as a Western hero. He directed, produced, and starred in the film, which also features impeccable performances by Morgan Freeman, Richard Harris, and Gene Hackman. The gorgeously photographed film tells the story of a reformed gunfighter, William Munny (Eastwood), who takes a break from pig-farming and single fatherhood to make one last score as a hired killer. The film debunks every Western movie myth in its portrayal of Munny as a man who can barely ride his horse or shoot his gun. He's haunted by every corpse he created, and even his beloved wife, who reformed him before dying of smallpox, returns to haunt him in his dreams. The film uses the graphic, excruciating violence that made Eastwood a macho man in the 1960s, but when he inflicts it on others, he does so with horror and with the knowledge of what he's doing. "The movie summarizes everything I feel about the Western," Eastwood told the *Los Angeles Times*. "The moral is the concern over gunplay."

Other rich details add to the complete demythologizing of the West, bringing the saga full circle. Among the mercenaries out to collect the $1,000 reward offered by vengeful prostitutes for killing a pair of cowhands who cut up a colleague's face is English Bob (Harris), who plays a bragging dandy of a gunslinger. He's accompanied by a Ned Buntline–style dime novelist who's penning his preposterously embellished adventures. Little Bill (Hackman), the outlaw-turned-sheriff who refuses to allow guns in Big Whiskey—home of the prostitutes and abusive ranch hands—brutally defeats Bob, wooing his biographer away in the process. When questioned about his own exploits, Munny is the opposite of self-aggrandizing; he credits whiskey for most of his previous daredevilry and feats of murder.

Still, the film has enough ambiguity and poetry to present a complex picture rather than a simplistic, facile one. According to Western film historians Rick Worland and Edward Countryman, "For two generations of moviegoers, Eastwood's weathered William Munny floats uneasily between the cynical Man With No Name who helped explode genre

clichés in Sergio Leone's Marxist anti-Westerns of the 1960s, and the rightist avenger 'Dirty Harry' Callahan of the 1970s and 1980s whose aura was eventually embraced by Ronald Reagan." They continue, "A powerful ambivalence about Munny's motives and actions results in a suggestively open-ended conclusion uncommon in post-*Star Wars* Hollywood."

Indeed, it was a coup for the man whose work has included directing *Bird*, an evocative portrait of his hero, bebop pioneer Charlie Parker. *Unforgiven* won four Academy Awards, including best picture, best director, best actor, and best supporting actor (Hackman). It was also the then sixty-one-year-old Eastwood's farewell to the West.

But not ours. *Unforgiven* showed that the Western is not an open-and-shut case that's been clichéd, torn apart, parodied, and re-created in every way possible. If a man who has given so much of his career to playing a cowboy leaves us asking questions, that's a good sign. As long as there is still a new way to look at the great American icon—that individualistic range rider on horseback—whether literally or figuratively, there will continue to be great Westerns.

Lawman Little Bill Daggett (Gene Hackman, opposite) and former gunslinger William Munny (Eastwood, above) are revealed as two sides of the same coin in a movie that questions every aspect of the Western myth and orthodoxy. It gains its authority from the fact that Eastwood—the modern icon of the West—wrote, directed, and produced it.

bibliography

Adams, Ramon F., *The Old-Time Cowhand* (New York: Collier, 1948, 1971)

Allen, Michael, *Rodeo Cowboys in the North American Imagination* (Lincoln: University of Nevada Press, 1998)

Aquila, Richard (editor), *Wanted Dead or Alive: The American West in Popular Culture* (Urbana/Chicago: University of Chicago Press, 1996)

Autry, Gene with Mickey Herskowitz, *Back in the Saddle Again* (New York: Doubleday, 1978)

Boylen, E.N. "Pink," *Episode of the West: The Pendleton Round-Up* (Pendleton, 1975)

Brownlow, Kevin, *The War, the West, and the Wilderness* (New York: Knopf, 1978)

Buscombe, Edward (editor), *The BFI Companion to the Western* (New York: Atheneum, 1998)

Cusic, Don, *Cowboys and the Wild West: An A–Z Guide from the Chisolm Trail to the Silver Screen* (New York: Facts on File, 1994)

Davis, Robert Murray, *Playing Cowboys: Low Culture and High Art in the Western* (Norman: University of Oklahoma Press, 1992)

Dillman, Bruce, *The Cowboy Handbook* (NE: Lone Prairie, 1994)

Everson, William K., *A Pictorial History of the Western Film* (New York: Citadel, 1969)

Farnum, Allen L., *Pawnee Bill's Historic Wild West* (PA, Schiffer, 1992)

Fayard, Judy, "Who Can Stand 32,580 Seconds of Clint Eastwood?" *Life* (July 23, 1971)

Fenin, George N. and William K. Everson, *The Western: From Silents to Cinerama* (New York: The Orion Press, 1962)

Forbis, William H. and the editors of Time-Life Books, *The Cowboy* (Alexandria: Time-Life, 1973)

Frayling, Christopher, *Sergio Leone: Something to Do with Death* (London: Faber and Faber, 2000)

George-Warren, Holly and Michelle Freedman, *How the West Was Worn* (New York: Harry N. Abrams, 2001)

Gilchriest, Gail, *The Cowgirl Companion* (New York: Hyperion, 1993)

Gordon, Alex, "The Western" (1992); Green, Douglas B., "The Singing Cowboy: An American Dream," *Journal of Country Music*, volume 7

Hake, Ted, *Hake's Guide to Cowboy Character Collectibles* (PA: Wallace-Homestead, 1994); *Happy Trails* (Rhino Entertainment, 1998)

Havinghurst, Walter, *Annie Oakley of the Wild West* (Lincoln: University of Nebraska Press, 1954)

Heide, Robert and John Gilman, *Box-Office Buckaroos* (New York: Abbeville Press, 1982)

Johnson, Cecil, *Guts: Legendary Black Rodeo Cowboy Bill Pickett* (TX: Summit, 1994)

Katz, William Loren, *Black Women of the Old West* (New York: Atheneum, 1995)

Kitses, Demetrius John, *Horizons West: Anthony Mann, Budd Boetticher, Sam Peckinpah* (Thames and Hudson, 1969)

Lahue, Kelton C., *Winners of the West: The Sagebrush Heroes of the Silent Screen* (New York: Castle Books, 1971)

Lahue, Kelton C., *Riders of the Range: The Sagebrush Heroes of the Sound Screen* (New York: Castle Books, 1973)

Lamar, Howard R., *The New Encyclopedia of the American West* (New Haven: Yale University Press, 1998)

LeSueur, Charlie, *The Legends Live On: Interviews with the Cowboy Stars of the Silver Screen* (AZ: Norseman, 1999)

Logsdon, Guy, Mary Rogers, and William Jacobson, *Saddle Serenaders* (Salt Lake City: Gibbs-Smith, 1995)

McBride, Joseph and Michael Wilmington, *John Ford* (New York: DaCapo, 1975)

Morris, Edmund, *The Rise of Theodore Roosevelt* (New York: Modern Library, 2001, 1979)

Oermann, Robert K., "The Queen of the West," Country Music, August 2001

"101 Ranch Real Wild West" show program, 1912

O'Neal, Bill, *Tex Ritter: America's Most Beloved Cowboy* (TX: Eakin, 1998)

Parker, James W., *All Along the Chisholm Trail* (OK, 1988)

Phillips, Robert W. *Singing Cowboy Stars* (Salt Lake City: Gibbs Smith, 1994)

Richards, Larry, *African American Films Through 1959* (NC: McFarland, 1998)

Rogers, Roy and Dale with Jane and Michael Stern, *Happy Trails: Our Life Story* (New York: Fireside, 1994)

Rogers Jr., Roy, with Karen Ann Wojahn, *Growing Up with Roy and Dale* (CA: Regal, 1986)

Rothel, Daniel, *The Gene Autry Book* (NC: Empire, 1998)

Rothel, Daniel, *The Roy Rogers Book* (NC: Empire, 1996)

Rothel, Daniel, *Those Great Cowboy Sidekicks* (NC: Empire, 2001)

Sampson, Henry T., *Blacks in Black and White: A Source Book on Black Film* (NJ: Scarecrow Press, 1995)

Sandler, Martin W., *Cowboys: A Library of Congress Book* (New York: HarperCollins, 1995)

Savage, Candace, *Cowgirls* (Berkeley: Ten Speed Press, 1996)

Seagraves, Anne, *Daughters of the West* (ID: Wesanne, 1996)

Seagraves, Anne, *Sing Cowboy Sing* (Rhino Entertainment, 1997)

Slotkin, Richard, *Gunfighter Nation: The Myth of the Frontier in Twentieth-Century America* (New York: Atheneum, 1992)

Stern, Jane and Michael, *Way Out West* (New York: HarperCollins, 1993)

Trachtman, Paul and the editors of Time-Life Books, *The Gunfighters* (VA: Time-Life, 1974)

Tuska, Jon, *The Filming of the West* (New York: Doubleday, 1976)

Ward, Fay E., *The Cowboy at Work* (New York: Hastings House, 1958)

White, John I., *Git Along, Little Dogies: Songs and Songmakers of the American West* (Urbana/Chicago, University of Illinois Press, 1989)

Wills, Garry, *John Wayne's America: The Politics of Celebrity* (New York: Simon & Schuster, 1997)

Wilson, R.L., with Greg Martin, *Buffalo Bill's Wild West: An American Legend* (New York: Random House, 1998)

Wister, Owen, *The Virginian* (New York: Macmillan, 1902, 1929)

Yoggy, Gary A. (editor), *Back in the Saddle: Essays on Western Film and Television Actors* (NC: McFarland, 1997)

index

PICTURE CREDITS

Every effort has been made to trace copyright holders and obtain permission. The publishers apologize for any omissions and would be pleased to make any necessary changes at subsequent printings.

Cameron Collection: 27, 28, 32, 36t, 157. **Corbis/Bettman Archive:** 6/7, 9, 10, 11t, 13b, 15, 16/17, 24, 26/27, 33, 37, 38, 41l, 42, 43, 49r, 54, 55, 88, 92, 95b, 107, 128, 130, 134, 137, 140t, 159t. **Corbis:** 8, 19 both, 20, 21, 22, 25 Buddy Mays, 30 Medford Historical Society Coll., 34/35, 36b Hulton-Deutsch Coll., 76b, 127, 132 both, 136 Carl & Ann Purcell, 136tr Christine Osborne, 136bl Catherine Karrow. **Photographs Courtesy the Kobal Collection:** 45, 48, 49l, 50, 51, 57, 59, 60, 61, 62, 63, 68, 69, 75, 76t, 79, 84, 85, 87, 89, 90, 97, 100, 102, 107 inset, 108, 109, 111, 112, 116, 117, 118 inset, 126, 133, 162, 171, 172, 174b, 193. © 20th Century Fox: 120, 153 Kobal, 178 Kobal, 179 Kobal, 214, 218t Kobal. © Boss/3P/JACS: 91 Kobal. © CBS/TV: 159b Kobal, 191, 196, 197m, 200 MGM. © Columbia Films: 148 Kobal, 152b Kobal, 185 Kobal. © Edison: 44 Kobal, 46/47 Kobal. © Famous Players Lasky: 53 Kobal, 58 Kobal. © Fox Films: 66/67 Kobal, 102 both, 143 Kobal. © Grey Fox/Mercury/Canadian Film/CVLP: 215b Kobal. © Hollywood Pictures Cinergi: 218b. © Jolly/Constantin/Ocean: 198, 205. © Orion Pictures Corporation: 212 both Kobal, 217 Kobal. © P.E.A.: 202/3 Kobal. © Paramount Films: 2 Kobal, 40b Kobal, 64/65 Kobal, 103, 104 Kobal, 115 inset Kobal, 139, 146, 163 Kobal, 177, 180, 182/183 Kobal, 194/195 TV/NBC. © Republic: 80 Kobal, 81b Kobal, 82 Kobal, 105 Kobal, 106 Kobal, 113, 119 Kobal, 121, 166 Kobal, 167 Kobal. © Tristar: 219 Kobal. © United Artists: 70/71 Kobal, 125 Kobal, 140b & 141 Stanley Kramer Kobal, 144, 145, 149 Kobal, 174t Kobal, 190, 199, 200/201 Kobal, 209 Kobal, 216t Kobal, 216b

Kobal. © Universal Pictures: 98/99 Kobal, 138 Kobal, 151 Kobal, 175, 184 Kobal, 208 Kobal, 210 Kobal. © Warner Bros: 52 MGM Kobal, 72 MGM Kobal, 73 RKO Kobal, 77 Kobal, 83 Kobal, 101 RKO Kobal, 150 MGM/Cinerama Kobal, 152t Kobal, 155 Kobal, 160/161 RKO Kobal, 164 RKO Kobal, 165 RKO Kobal, 173, 176 Kobal, 181,197 TV, 206 Warner 7 Arts, 207 MGM Kobal, 211 Kobal, 213b, 216tr, 220 both, 221.

AUTHOR ACKNOWLEDGMENTS

Cowboy benefited from the insights of numerous Western aficionados. Alex Gordon generously offered his encyclopedic knowledge of film history. Others whose input was invaluable include James Austin, Clare and Todd Butler, Michelle Freedman, Charles Leland, Deb O'Nair, James W. Parker, Melissa Reynolds, Mike Evans, Sophie Collins, Caroline Earle, Kate Halloran, the Autry Museum of Western Heritage's Marva Felchlin and Susan Van deVey, Autry Entertainment's Karla Buhlman and Maxine Hansen, and the Phoenicia Library's gracious staff, including Hilary, Molly, Debbie, and Violet. I'm also indebted to my posse of mentors: Sarah Lazin, Ben Fong-Torres, Anthony DeCurtis, and Patty Romanowski. Words cannot express my gratitude to my grandmother Brownie George; my late parents Martha and Alvis George; my brothers Owen and Robert George; my aunts Frances Spratt, Jean Holland, and Lou Wolfe; my cousin Ann Griffin and her family; my amazing equestrienne mother-in-law Mary Lucchese; and my incredibly supportive and loving husband and son Robert and Jackson Warren, who didn't mind—too much—watching hundreds of Westerns. And, finally, muchas gracias to the cowboys and cowgirls of the real—and reel—West.